Presented To:

_____

From:

_____

Date:

_____

THE ART OF
COMMUNICATION

THE ART OF
COMMUNICATION

YOUR **COMPETITIVE** EDGE

JIM STOVALL
& RAY H. HULL, PhD

For more information on foreign distribution, call 717-530-2122.

Reach us on the Internet: www.soundwisdom.com.

Sound Wisdom
P.O. Box 310
Shippensburg, PA 17257-0310

ISBN 13 TP: 978-0-7684-1060-0
ISBN 13 HC: 978-0-7684-0959-8
ISBN 13 eBook: 978-0-7684-0960-4

For Worldwide Distribution, Printed in the U.S.A.
1 2 3 4 5 6 7 8 / 20 19 18 17 16

Contents

PREFACE

Those who communicate well have a competitive advantage in their personal and professional lives. Of course, everyone communicates. Even if we try not to, it remains that we are, in one way or another, still communicating. The "silent treatment" that we may be attempting to give another person is still communicating—that perhaps we are unhappy with the other person, or that we have nothing more to say on the matter. However, we are, indeed, still communicating.

Communication manifests itself in a myriad of ways. But, whether we intend to or not, it remains that we are still communicating. As we, the authors, say in this book, communication is irretrievable; that is, we cannot take words back once they are uttered. No matter how much we may wish we had not said them, they cannot be retrieved. We can feel badly that we said those words, but we cannot erase them or the possible hurt. The best we can do is apologize.

We entitled this book *The Art of Communication* for a reason. The reason? Communication, if done well, is an art. It is an art that can be continually refined throughout our lifetime. The problem is, however, that it is too frequently engaged in without much thought. As we find with any art form, it can be seen or heard as refined and appealing, or it can cause one to wonder how or why it was put on display in a public place!

In response to the possibility that the latter is what you are experiencing in your own communicative life, this book is divided into two components. One half of the chapters are written to present the more technical, or should we say, the more informational aspects of communication by Ray H. Hull, PhD. Every other chapter throughout the book describes in beautiful ways, by author Jim Stovall, how communication manifests itself in our daily lives.

We hope that you enjoy this book, and the "art of communication" that we are sharing with you. If read carefully and completely, it will give you a competitive edge in your personal and professional life. As Aristotle once said, "A successful person is one who communicates well."

Introduction

By Jim Stovall

My Dear Reader:

I want to thank you as you have greatly honored my coauthor Dr. Ray Hull and me with the investment of your hard-earned money and valuable time that you have made in this book.

I have written approximately 30 previous books and have consistently avoided coauthors like the plague with a few rare exceptions. This book will be another of those rare exceptions because Dr. Ray Hull is a rare exception himself and uniquely qualified to teach both you and me the vital and intricate principles that govern the universe of communication.

I met Ray at an annual conference attended by hundreds of talented and dedicated people who manage special education projects funded by the U.S. Department of Education. My company, Narrative Television Network, is involved in one of these projects that makes educational television and video programming accessible for blind and visually impaired students across the country. Jo Ann McCann is the project officer for the U.S. Department of Education who oversees the work done by NTN and many other organizations involved in this important work to make the educational process accessible to all children regardless of their disabilities.

I consider Jo Ann to be a great friend and valued colleague, but I will admit when she suggested that we attend a session on hearing disabilities and audiology conducted by Dr. Ray Hull, whom I had never heard of, I was a bit perplexed; however, over the years, I have come to understand that there is generally a method to Jo Ann's madness, so I withheld judgment and attended the session. Dr. Hull's hour-long lecture was compelling and intriguing but seemed to have nothing to do with our work for blind and visually impaired children at the Narrative Television Network.

Although I have been totally blind for more than 25 years, I still retain a number of visual images and memories. Among them are the visual optic puzzles that might appear at first glance to be an elm tree, but if you stare at it long enough, it is revealed to be an image of six presidents of the United States. There is a fascinating moment of revelation when the image instantly changes, and the tree disappears as the presidents are revealed. A similar moment often occurs in real life. My late, great friend and colleague Dr. Stephen Covey called this moment a paradigm shift.

One moment I was thinking that Ray Hull's work had nothing to do with mine, and Jo Ann had obviously led me astray, and the next moment I knew that Dr. Ray Hull's work was at the very core of making our work at the Narrative Television Network everything I had hoped and dreamed it would be in the lives of countless blind and visually impaired children seeking a quality education and a fulfilling life. Our work, quite simply, describes the visual elements of a program by inserting brief lines of narration between the dialogue of a movie, television show, or educational video. Helping people hear what they can't see so that they can visualize images utilizing their ears is the essence of the art of communication. When you only have a few seconds to describe a whole world of visual images, you want to communicate concisely, effectively, and completely.

I knew Dr. Ray Hull's work in the field of audiology could revolutionize communication with blind and visually impaired young people struggling to compete with their four senses in a world of people with five senses.

Dr. Ray Hull is a master of communication and treasures it as only someone who didn't have it and fought to gain it can.

Raymond H. Hull, PhD, is currently the Professor of Communication Sciences and Disorders Coordinator in the Doctor of Audiology program at the College of Health Professions at Wichita State University. Prior to that, he was Chair of the Department of Communication Disorders at the University of Northern Colorado for 12 years. He has also held administrative posts within the graduate school, being responsible for graduate program review and evaluation both at that university and Wichita State University for eight years, and he was the Director of Planning and

Budget for the Office of the President for seven years at the University of Northern Colorado. He has held administrative posts both at the University of Northern Colorado in the College of Health and Human Sciences, the Office of the President, and at Wichita State University through the graduate school. He is a successful grant writer with over $12 million in funded federal grants.

His background in the field of neuroscience of human communication began with his college degree in public speaking, drama, and radio/television broadcast, and then moved into graduate work in disorders of human communication, followed by a doctorate in audiology and the neurosciences of human communication that involved a combined doctoral degree from the University of Colorado School of Medicine and the University of Denver. He works extensively in coaching the art of interpersonal communication in professional life—the nature of interpersonal communication that supports success in one's personal and professional life—and is a sought-after speaker on that topic both nationally and internationally.

Dr. Hull is the past chair of the American Speech-Language-Hearing Association Committee on Communication Problems of the Aging and is a past member of the ASHA Committee on Governmental Regulations. In 2008, he was selected for membership on the ASHA/ETS National Audiology Praxis Advisory Committee. He has also had membership on the ASHA Advisory Committee for the project on Upgrading Services to Communicatively Impaired Persons funded by the Bureau of Health Professions, PHS. He is a member of the Advisory, Guidance, and Evaluation Team of the ASHA Project on Satellite Training on Communicative Behavior of Older Americans,

Administration on Aging, DHHS. He has been vice chair of the ASHA Audiology Advisory Committee and is a current member of the ASHA Audiology Advisory Counsel, among other national and state appointments.

Dr. Hull has been editorial advisor to the *American Journal of Audiology, Ear and Hearing; The Journal of the American Auditory Society; The Journal of the American Academy of Audiology;* and *The Journal of International Audiology.*

He is sought after as a speaker/presenter, and has authored and presented over 200 major presentations and workshops across the U.S., Canada, South America, and Europe on the art of communication in professional practice, talking to children, auditory assessment, environmental design, central auditory processing, and hearing rehabilitation for children and adults with impaired hearing.

The foregoing academic accomplishments, professional achievements, and honors make Ray an eminent expert in the field of communication but does not fully explain why I wanted to coauthor this book with him.

Four of my novels have been turned into major motion pictures with two more in production at this writing. I believe storytelling is a highly impactful communication tool, and I am grateful for the opportunity to share my stories via print and the silver screen with millions around the world; but if I had drafted Ray Hull's true-life story as a potential novel or movie script, New York publishers and Hollywood movie producers would have simply laughed at me.

Ray Hull grew up in the figurative and geographical heart of our country. When Ray was very young, he was called a "pretty boy" by those who saw him, so I suppose appearance can disguise disabilities to some degree. Among his recollections that he was different was when he was six years old and in the first grade. As Ray was walking the four blocks from his elementary school to his home one afternoon, three bullies from his school met him about halfway. He did not know their names, but he knew they were tough by reputation. They were laughing and teasing him because he was a "stutterer."

"He talks funny!" they said as they knocked him down and walked away.

After Ray recovered his senses, he picked himself up off the sidewalk and ran home crying. The teasing was occurring with greater frequency, and Ray was angry at those who teased him and angry at himself for, obviously, being so different.

Before and after that incident, Ray's parents tried to offer their own brand of therapy to "cure" what they called "stammering." "Slow down, think about what you're saying, and sing your words," were among their "cures." Of course, none of those worked, and Ray's dysfluencies became worse as his fears and inability to say his name or answer the telephone without severe stuttering "blocks" continued and strengthened. The stuttering blocks had become so severe that they prevented all vocalization from being emitted. Attempting to force vocalizations only resulted in a sustained guttural vowel "a" as in *daaaaaaaa* as Ray would, for example, attempt to utter the word "dog."

What kept Ray going, however, was the realization that he did not stutter when he talked to his dog, Laddie. So, he talked frequently to him. He also did not stutter when he talked to the calves he was preparing for the 4H fair, or when he was feeding the cows each morning and evening on his family's farm. Ray was always fluent.

And being quite musical vocally, Ray was also aware that he did not stutter when he sang. He reasoned then that, perhaps, he did not *have* to stutter, that perhaps there was nothing organically wrong with him. Maybe if he could get over his fear of talking, or rather his fear of the embarrassments that resulted from stuttering, maybe it would subside. *But how does one do that?* he wondered.

So, with the knowledge that there were times when he did not stutter, Ray set out to "cure" himself from the stuttering that he considered to be a dark cloud that was with him wherever he went and whenever he spoke.

Ray's first course of action was to begin placing himself in situations that required talking and to do that as many times as it took to begin to experience success. He reasoned, correctly or incorrectly, that if he were occasionally successful in speaking with greater fluency, then those successes might breed further success.

These included:

High school plays: Perhaps due to Ray's youth as a high school student and perhaps with more youthful bravery than good sense, he had what he thought was a good rationale for auditioning for acting roles in plays. His rationale was that if a part in a play was offered to him and he accepted, he couldn't walk off the stage during a production because the other actors would be depending on him to say his lines, and say them correctly. Ray auditioned for every play he could during his years in high school. His freshman year, he was given the role of Johnny Appleseed in the musical by the same name. He could sing and had a rather high tenor, near-soprano, pubescent voice, so the role fit. Thankfully, it was a non-speaking role. All Ray had to do was sing two solos, and he sang fluently. It was a great morale booster when he heard the applause from the audience.

Speech 101: Success can have roadblocks. On the first day of a required high school course that was entitled Speech 101, the teacher asked each student to introduce her or himself. As Ray's turn became imminent, his face and larynx began to tighten in preparation. As he feared would happen, he stood by his desk, opened his mouth, and nothing came out. Ray's vocal folds were tightly closed, and the stuttering block was both massive and embarrassing.

"Mah…mah…mah…mah…," trying desperately to say, "My name is…," was all he could utter.

Students around him began to snicker quietly. He quickly sat back at his desk not wanting to look at anyone.

Ray's teacher quietly said, "Thank you, Raymond," and went on to the next student who spoke beautifully.

Becoming a radio disc jockey: Ray's junior year in high school, he did something that he didn't think he would ever have the courage to do. Ray drove to a local radio station after school one day and nervously asked the secretary at the front desk if he could see the station manager. She consented, and from a script that he had written ahead of time to help him speak as fluently as possible, Ray asked the station manager if he could have 30 minutes every afternoon, Monday through Friday, for a rock-and-roll disc jockey show.

The station manager had apparently thought about it before, because he finally said, "Yes, I think we might try that. We'll see how it goes. You will begin next Monday at 4:00 p.m. Be here at 3:30 p.m. to prepare. A studio engineer will run the control board for you for a few days until you get the hang of it."

So, Ray had three days to prepare.

The show was eventually expanded to an hour, from 4:00 to 5:00 p.m. Monday through Friday as its popularity grew. For the first few weeks, Ray spoke and introduced songs by reading from a script he wrote each day. Eventually, the script was placed aside, and as long as Ray was speaking into a microphone and there was not an audience on the other side of the glass studio window, he was more fluent than he could ever remember being.

Intercollegiate oratory. As Ray entered college, he continued to place himself in situations that required talking. During his senior year, among those places was intercollegiate oratory in which the competitors were to prepare and give 12- to 15-minute orations from memory. The required topic was *Achieving World Peace.* With the help of his forensics coach who was not sure that he should enter the competition, Ray wrote his oration and rehearsed it until he was able to present it from memory.

The day of the state competition, Ray was to drive to one of the large universities in his home state of Kansas, about 90 miles away from his farm. It was the middle of winter, and it was snowing, but he drove there anyway.

After arriving and walking through a grassy field of mud and slush, Ray finally arrived at the correct building, but the lower one-third of the pants of his new blue suit as well as his new shoes were covered with mud. Ray hurried to the room where the competition was being held and slowly opened the door. As he did, he discovered that the final competitor was just finishing his oration. When the final competitor concluded, Ray asked the judges if there was still time for him to present. The judges conferred and said that he could. Ray then asked if he could go to a restroom. After washing off as much mud as he could, Ray walked without hesitation to the front of the speakers' room, faced the judges and the other orators and their coaches who were seated near them, and without forethought began his 15-minute oration from memory. Ray was so concerned about being late and the appearance of his shoes and slacks he did not have time to build any level of anxiety and was, therefore, fairly fluent. If there were dysfluencies, Ray tried to use them as pauses for purposes of emphasis.

At the conclusion of his oration, Ray simply thanked the judges, walked from the room, and drove the 90 miles back to his farm in central Kansas. Ray was embarrassed by what he thought had been a poor performance, but he had completed his oration in its entirety and felt that he had done his best in spite of his muddy slacks and shoes and his near panic as a result of being late for the competition.

When Ray arrived home at his family's farm, it was late in the evening. At about 9:00 p.m., the telephone rang, and his mother answered. She said that Ray's forensics coach wanted to speak with him. As he put the receiver to his ear, his coach spoke and was almost beside himself with excitement. Ray was informed that he had won first place in the Kansas State Intercollegiate Men's Oratory Competition, the first time it had happened to anyone at his small college. It was difficult for Ray to believe what had just happened, that he was the best orator of the best from the colleges and universities in his state. It was a grand achievement in the life of a stutterer.

Ray was absolutely floating in fluency!

Because Ray had won the State Intercollegiate Men's Oratory competition, he was to move on to the regional and national competitions. As he was rehearsing at home in his bedroom, Ray slowly began to experience the return of stuttering blocks. He is still not sure why that occurred. Perhaps fatigue or fear of failure. They began slowly, but as his fears grew, the all-too-familiar stuttering blocks quickly grew in both frequency and intensity and then increased with a vengeance. Ray could not talk. The fears and the stuttering blocks had returned, but in light of his previous successes, Ray was not going to give up and spend his life as a stutterer.

So upon graduation from college, Ray decided to go on to graduate school into the field of radio/television broadcast, a return to an area in which he had previously experienced success. He had chosen one of the few universities that offered a graduate degree in those fields.

During the first summer, he was required to take an introductory course entitled *Human Communication Disorders*. During that course, Ray became fascinated by the variety of disorders of communication that can affect children and adults. When the class entered the topic of fluency disorders, Ray reluctantly accepted the invitation to talk about how it feels to be a stutterer. When he went to the front of the classroom to make his presentation, he was surprised that he was not dysfluent at any time while he spoke about the feelings one experiences when confronted with the problem of stuttering. After that presentation, Ray reasoned that, perhaps, in talking about his feelings regarding the problem of stuttering and not attempting to hide them or disguise them, the pressure to be fluent was absent; therefore, fluency increased.

At that point, Ray's stuttering extinguished to the degree that he was essentially fluent most of the time, and he has been since that summer. Everything seemed to boil down to the fact that Ray's original plan was the best one. Success does breed success! That has been and continues to be his premise. At this time in his adult life, he is still a stutterer, but he is able to control it to the point that it is unnoticeable. If a stuttering block does occur, he uses it as a pause for emphasis in regard to what he is saying, and he doesn't worry about it.

My grandfather always told me that a person with experience never has to take a backseat to a person with a theory. Dr. Ray Hull has both theory and experience relating to the field of communication.

In this book, Ray will be sharing the principles behind communication, and I will be sharing—in alternate chapters—the practical, real-world reality of communication based on my experience as a speaker, author, movie producer, TV executive, and syndicated columnist.

It is true that no person is an island. Success in our personal or professional lives requires us to depend on and interact with other people. We may have the greatest hopes, dreams, goals, and aspirations, but unless we can communicate our vision, we are doomed to fail.

It is our fervent hope that, within these pages, you will learn how to improve your communication, and thereby improve your life.

Jim Stovall

2015

CHAPTER 1

THE ART OF COMMUNICATION

Introduction

Successful communication is an art. It is an art, but it is also a science. There are so many intricate, or perhaps I should say delicate, components that are involved in interpersonal communication, it is a wonder that it is ever actually considered to be successful.

On the other hand, the many components of successful interpersonal communication can be learned. That is the purpose of this book: to instruct the reader regarding the many elements of this oftentimes misunderstood and nearly mystical system of purely human interaction that is called verbal and nonverbal communication.

Why Is It Important to Study Interpersonal Communication?

Much of what we do in our day-to-day interactions with colleagues, friends, significant others and the public involves communication in one form or another. As we work to be successful in our occupations and our personal relationships, or as we strive for advancement in any organizational structure, it is imperative that we become familiar with the processes involved in effective interpersonal communication and its potential impact on all that we do.

Importantly, interpersonal communication goes beyond talking. Much beyond simply talking, interpersonal communication includes the creation of an "atmosphere" of communication that results in positive and constructive interaction with others.

The better we are in this aspect of our life, the more successful we will become. All else being equal, it is often the basis upon which we choose our physician, our dentist, our favorite place to eat, the family member everyone goes to when there is a problem, our place of worship, the politicians we vote for, our child's babysitter, and even our hairdresser!

We are drawn to those who make us feel most comfortable, who communicate with us in a positive and supportive manner, who seem to understand our problems, those we trust, and who we would go to in times of difficulty. It is, in the end, what separates those who are successful in their life and in their work from those who are less successful. It signifies who we are, or who we want to be. In fact, a Wall Street Journal Corporate Recruiters Survey lists the ten most important attributes that high-level recruiters look for, and "communication/interpersonal skills" is consistently found at the top of the list. Skill in communication is critically important to our success in any field. So, what does it involve?

Importantly...

Interpersonal communication not only involves what we *say*, but very importantly what we *do* in our communicative inter-actions with others. What we *do* may involve our manner of dress, our body language, gestures, manner of eye contact, and personal grooming. In many instances, the nonverbal aspects of communication are not only important, but are frequently more important than what we *say*. The intended result of those verbal and nonverbal interactions may be a change in attitudes, behav-iors, or beliefs of the person with whom we are communicating. Or, perhaps it can result in the development of creative resolutions through constructive problem solving when otherwise there may have been conflict. But, the characteristics of unpredictability and the inherent complexities of interpersonal communication make it particularly challenging!

Why Do Some People Seem to Have Difficulty Communicating Well with Others?

In the paragraph above, I said that the characteristics of unpredictability and the inherent complexities of interpersonal communication make that important activity particularly challenging. For some people, the complexities that are inherent in interpersonal communication are the catalyst for the difficulties that they experience in their ability to communicate effectively with others. Why is that? It is because some people seem to have difficulty attending to all of the complex events that can occur during communicative exchanges, or they have not been formally or even informally prepared in this complex aspect of human behavior. Their personality or behaviors may be getting in the way of positive and constructive interpersonal interaction with others. Or, during their earlier years, they may have been exposed to poor models of communication.

As I tell my patients who have difficulty hearing, "Whether we want to or not, we live in a world of people who do not communicate well." I continue by saying, "But, we also live in a world of people who do not possess the knowledge or skill to be good communicators!" It is simply that many people possess communication habits that are much less than desirable, and all of us, whether we possess excellent hearing or not, may have difficulty understanding what they are saying.

For example, I am witness to people who speak with such speed that most listeners' central nervous systems simply cannot keep up with the words that are being uttered. Therefore, it is difficult to understand what those people are saying because the speed at which they are speaking results in their use of only partial words. Or, perhaps their ability to respond to us in a positive and constructive manner when we are attempting to communicate with them is lacking. Or, their ability to listen well to what we are saying is less than desirable. Perhaps they do not attend to us when we are speaking to them, or have poor eye contact, or less than desirable body language as they interact with us. Perhaps their manner of standing or sitting while communicating with us is distracting, or they do not exhibit the poise and attentiveness that assures us that they are actively listening to what we are saying. (The subject of "active listening" will be discussed later in this book.)

However, in order to be successful in our daily interactions with those with whom we communicate, whether it be in matters of love, family, business, public speaking engagements, or even political campaigns, it is imperative that we learn how to effectively engage in this complex but important aspect of our life that is called "human communication."

Does It Mean That I'm a Poor Communicator If I Don't Communicate Perfectly?

That is a question I am asked quite frequently. Here is my response. Effective interpersonal communication does not mean always communicating perfectly. I have never met anyone who communicates perfectly. Rather it means being able to constructively create and convey appropriate responses to those with whom we are communicating, and to perhaps identify and explain creative solutions that are acceptable to them. It means motivating others to positive change through direct verbal interaction, nonverbal interaction (what we don't say), our body language, and through a *positive* atmosphere of communication that we create.

I like the phrase "positive atmosphere of communication." The reason I like it is because it provides a framework for communication that is constructive and successful. Rather than communicating perfectly, I like to think in terms of communicating *constructively*—or *meaningfully*. When we communicate constructively, we are more apt to be communicating in a meaningful way.

So, in the End, What Is It?

Recently I read a well-written treatise on communication. It said, in part, "interpersonal communication is the process by which people exchange information, feelings, and meaning through verbal and nonverbal messages." That is a very straightforward definition.

The authors continue, "Interpersonal communication is not just about what is actually said—the language used—but *how* it is said and the nonverbal messages sent through tone of voice, facial expressions, gestures and body language."[1] Again, very straightforward!

The authors explain that when two or more people are in the same place and are aware of each other's presence, one way or another communication is taking place, no matter how subtle or unintentional or how poorly it is being handled.

Is Speech Necessary?

Using speech is not necessary. Without speech, the listener may be observing the use of cues of posture, facial expression, and dress to form an impression of the other's role, emotional state, personality and/or intentions. Although no communication may be intended, people receive messages through nonverbal behaviors (nonverbal communication will be discussed later in this book).

Some Principles of Interpersonal Communication

The authors continue by giving principles of interpersonal communication that I personally like. Most of these will be addressed throughout this book in different chapters, but they are listed here. They govern the effectiveness of communication. However, as the authors say, even though these principles are generally quite simple, they will often take a lifetime to master. They are presented as follows:

1. Interpersonal Communication Is Not Optional

We may, at times, try not to communicate; but *not* communicating is not an option. In fact, the harder we try not to communicate, the more we are communicating! By not communicating we are communicating *something*, perhaps that we are shy, perhaps that we are angry or sulking, perhaps that we are too busy to talk. Ignoring somebody is communicating with them. We may not tell them we are ignoring them, but through our nonverbal means of communication we make that apparent.

Again, nonverbal communication can be just as, and many times more powerful than, the words that we use. Our body posture and position and our eye contact (or lack of it) are all important. Even the smallest and most subtle of mannerisms communicate something to others.

2. Communication Is Irreversible

Interpersonal communication is irreversible. Perhaps we can wish we had not said something. We feel a sense of regret and apologize for something we said, but we can't take it back. We often behave and therefore communicate to others based on previous communication encounters. But, those encounters may or may not be appropriate points of reference. Because of these stereotypes, when we communicate with people, we can carry with us certain preconceptions of what the other person is thinking or how they are likely to behave. We may also have ideas about the outcome of the conversation before it even begins as a result of our pre-knowledge of the person or the circumstances in which the conversation is taking place.

We need to start all interpersonal communication with an open mind; listen to what is being said rather than hearing what we *expect* to hear. As a result, we are less likely to be misunderstood or say things that we later regret.

3. Endless Complexity

No form of communication is simple. There are many reasons why communication is taking place, how it is taking place, and how messages are being broadcast and received. Variables in communication, such as language, environment, and distraction as well as the individuals involved in communicating, all have an effect on how messages are sent, received, and interpreted. Interpersonal communication involves an extremely complex mixture of human behaviors that are sometimes difficult to comprehend, or at least to manage.

When we communicate verbally, we swap words—words that, even subtly, have different meanings to different people in different contexts. We can communicate the same thing to several different individuals, and each person may have a different understanding or interpretation of the message.

At any point in communication, any misunderstanding, regardless of how small it may seem, will have an effect on the message that is being received.

4. *The Context of Communication*

Communication happens for a reason. To help avoid misunderstandings, and therefore communicate more effectively, it is important that the context of the communication is understood by all. Why is the communication happening? It is important that participants are on the same "wavelength" so that they understand why the communication is occurring. We may think that "why" is clearly evident, but it may not be clear to all who are involved. There are things that can get in the way. Those can include the following:

Timing

Timing is fundamental to successful communication. As well as considering a suitable time to hold a conversation, you should make sure that there is enough time to cover all that is needed, including time to clarify and negotiate. For example, talking to employees about a strategic decision five minutes before they were planning to leave the office for the day would probably not be as successful as having the same conversation the following morning.

Location

It should be fairly obvious that communication is going to be less effective if it is conducted in a noisy, uncomfortable, or busy place. Such places have many distractions and often a lack of privacy. Depending on the reason for the conversation, a quieter environment may be appropriate, or perhaps a more casual conversation during lunchtime, or a relaxing conversation over a late afternoon cocktail at a local club may even be appropriate.

Why Is The Conversation Taking Place?

We can develop misconceptions and false assumptions regarding communication and why it is taking place. When communicating we may assume that all parties know what we are talking about, and we may even think that we know the other person's views and opinions regarding the purpose of the conversation. Most disturbing to others involved in the conversation, we "know" that our opinion is right and theirs is wrong. These can all be detrimental to constructive conversations in meetings, or even a street-side conversation, and must be avoided at all costs.

In Summary: In This Book

All of the elements above play a role in communication, and each of them can be a boon or a detriment to its success. Those and many others will be discussed in this book, and all are important as we learn about the components of constructive and successful communication.

Those will include:

- The art of communication that can influence outcomes of meetings and interviews

- The art of nonverbal communication

- The art of constructive listening

- The art of public speaking

- The art of public relations and image—impressing our clients and customers

- The art of conflict resolution

Note

1. "Interpersonal Communication Skills," Skills You Need, What Is Interpersonal Communication? accessed August 12, 2015, http://www.skillsyouneed.com/ips/interpersonal-communication.html.

CHAPTER 2

THE ARENA OF COMMUNICATION

It was one of those surreal moments that seems totally foreign to us, but at the same time somehow defines us.

I was standing backstage in a huge arena filled with 14,000 businesspeople who were somehow waiting to hear me speak. I was not thinking as much about what I was going to say as I was trying to remember how many steps it was to the front of the stage and where the podium was located. It was my first speech as a totally blind person.

I heard the authoritative voice of the master of ceremonies booming throughout the arena as he began my introduction. "In spite of blindness, Jim Stovall has been a National Olympic weight-lifting champion, a successful investment broker, the President of the Emmy Award-winning Narrative Television Network, and a highly sought-after author and platform speaker. He is the author of 30 books, including the best seller, *The Ultimate Gift*, which is now a major motion picture from 20th Century Fox starring James Garner and Abigail Breslin. Three of his other novels have also been made into movies with two more in production.

"Steve Forbes, president and CEO of *Forbes* magazine, says, 'Jim Stovall is one of the most extraordinary men of our era.'

"For his work in making television accessible to our nation's 13 million blind and visually impaired people, The President's Committee on Equal Opportunity selected Jim Stovall as the Entrepreneur of the Year. Jim Stovall has been featured in *The Wall Street Journal, Forbes* magazine, *USA Today*, and has been seen on *Good Morning America, CNN,* and *CBS Evening News.* He was also chosen as the International Humanitarian of the Year, joining Jimmy Carter, Nancy Reagan, and Mother Teresa as recipients of this honor."

As I stood there backstage trying to collect my thoughts, I remembered a time in my life when everything in that introduction, as well as the very thought of making the speech like I was getting ready to make, would have seemed as foreign to me as going to the moon. Communicating for over an hour with nothing between me and 14,000 people but a microphone seemed absurd and impossible in the moment.

I remembered as a young man that my greatest ambition in life had been nothing, more or less, than being an All-American football player and going into the NFL to make my living as a professional.

Communicating among and between football players is a very intricate and specialized system. In 21st century life when we meet a new person, we generally begin our communication by exchanging some simple information. We give our name and then we might inquire what the other person does and where they're from. In the football world, this is all accomplished by simply wearing a jersey. Your name is on the back of your jersey, your number indicates what you do as each position has different numbers, and the color of your jersey defines who you play for and, therefore, where you're from.

In the corporate world, we spend a lot of time, effort, and energy having meetings to determine what we're going to do, when it will be done, why we're going to do it, and which colleagues will perform what tasks. In a football huddle, within a few seconds using terms such as "blue 56 right stretch crossover on 2" tells each participant where they should be and what they should do in very specific detail.

The stereotypical "dumb jock" simply doesn't exist at least within the context of the sport they are playing. Football players know dozens of plays in various formations that create hundreds of variables, and depending on how the other team lines up, there can be literally thousands of permutations of each of the variables. All of this needs to be identified, understood, and acted upon in seconds or even fractions of seconds. This communication precision is possible because each member of the team agrees upon a very narrow and specific definition of terms. I've often thought the corporate world, the academic world, and life in general could be improved by taking a few communication lessons from football players.

My trajectory toward the NFL was interrupted one fall when I was preparing to go play another season of football. Each year before the season starts, all football players are required to get a thorough physical exam. I've often joked that "They want to make sure you're healthy before they take you out on the field and try to kill you."

That one particular day, the physical exam seemed to be taking a lot longer than I had remembered it being in previous years. The doctor ran several tests and called in a second physician to run some additional tests. Finally, they consulted with a third doctor, and eventually the three doctors took me down a long hall and sat me down at a conference table and then declared, "Jim, we're not sure why, and we're not sure when, but we do know that someday you're going to be totally blind, and there's nothing we can do about it."

This communication was brief, definite, and life-altering. I knew I was not going to go into the NFL and make my living as a football player. At that time and to this very day, there has never been a blind player in the NFL. I always like to tell my audiences jokingly, "Even though there's no blind players in the NFL, there are a few referees we're worried about."

I knew my football-playing days were over so I went back to the only job I had ever done before, which involved me being a laborer on a construction site.

The construction industry has a language and communication style of its own. There are terms used on a construction site you won't hear anywhere else, and virtually anything that can be communicated verbally to a construction worker can be communicated through signs done by the hands, arms, and body. Often, the construction site is so noisy that verbal communication is impossible, and this nonverbal construction sign language communication is important to get the job done properly; in a dangerous environment, it can actually mean the difference between life and death.

Just when I thought my athletic career was over, I was introduced to Olympic weightlifting. I thought, *This is a sport that a guy could compete in even if he were losing his sight or became totally blind.*

Olympic weightlifting is a sport that most Americans only think about every four years during the Olympic Games, but around the world it is a very popular sport all the time. I rapidly found myself competing with Russians, Eastern Europeans, South Americans, and athletes from Asia. While we could not readily communicate verbally, as elite athletes in a specific sport we all seemed to understand one another as our training and competitive routines were much the same, and we came to understand we all had much in common with one another.

In the midst of my weightlifting career, I enrolled in a local university and began my college experience. Academic settings have their own unique form of communication. In each field of study, a student has to learn a new vernacular. There are terms and nuances that are unique to every area of study. With all due respect to academicians and especially my esteemed coauthor, Dr. Hull, I believe that some communication within the academic arena is purposely archaic, obtuse, and difficult to understand or internalize. While there are certainly many exceptions to this rule, professors and professionals who study or work within a specific field need to understand that it is their role to make the complex simple through their communications, and it is not their role to make the simple complex.

I eventually graduated from the university with degrees in psychology and sociology. Studying human thought and human interaction creates a myriad of communication challenges. Describing our feelings verbally is one of the most difficult human tasks. Whether it's Sigmund Freud, William Shakespeare, or Edgar Allen Poe, they all became renowned through their prowess in masterfully communicating various feelings and emotions through their words.

In my late 20s, I finally experienced that fateful day the doctors had predicted. I woke up one morning and instantly realized I had lost the remainder of my sight. I had never realized before losing my vision how important sight was to verbal or written communication. Terms such as *yellow, large, vertical, bright*, and *beautiful* all come from using words to describe visual images. The day I lost my sight, I had no idea that these kinds of descriptions would become a big part of my personal and professional life.

I was age 29, and I had never met a blind person. I didn't have a clue what I was going to do with the rest of my life. I moved into this little 9- by 12-foot room in the back of my house, and I really fully intended to never leave that room again. The life I lead today would have seemed beyond impossible to me as I sat in my little 9 by 12-foot self-imposed prison.

Ironically, before I had lost my sight and began using that little room in the back of the house as my entire world, we had used it as our television room. Before I became blind, I was a huge fan of classic movies enjoying vintage stars such as John Wayne, Jimmy Stewart, Humphrey Bogart, and Katharine Hepburn. Sitting there as a blind person, becoming more distressed and discouraged each day, I knew that somewhere in the opposite corner of that room there was a TV, a VCR, and my classic movie collection.

One day, out of sheer boredom, I decided to play one of those old movies. I thought that I had seen them all so many times I should be able to just listen to the movie and follow along. I put on an old Humphrey Bogart detective film called *The Big Sleep*. Listening worked for a while as I could use my memories to visualize the various scenes in the movie, but then somebody shot somebody, and the car sped away, and I heard somebody scream, and I forgot the entire plot of that movie.

I got really frustrated and said, "Somebody ought to do something about that."

The next time you get frustrated and hear yourself utter those words, you just had a great idea. The only thing you need to do to have a great idea is to go through your daily routine, wait for something bad to happen, and ask yourself, "How could I have avoided that?" The answer to that question is a great idea. The only thing you've got to do to turn your idea into a great business is to ask one further question. "How could I help other people avoid that?" The answer to that question is a great business idea.

I believe the world will give you fame, fortune, and anything you want if you will help other people solve their problems.

Sitting there in my little 9 by 12-foot room, listening to the soundtrack of the movie I was unable to follow, I realized that if someone would add an extra sound track to movies, TV shows, and educational programming between the dialogue to describe the visual elements of the program, blind and visually impaired people could enjoy them. This thought was the beginning of my company the Narrative Television Network which, over the last 25 years, has made movies and television accessible to millions of blind and visually impaired Americans as well as countless more people around the world.

The idea of describing visual images to a blind person is not original with me. It is as old as the first blind person who had a friend or family member willing to verbally share the visual world with him. The process of describing or communicating visual elements through verbal cues is both an art and a science.

We have produced many thousands of hours of accessible movies, TV shows, and educational programs. While we are getting better at it every day, each time we improve the process, we realize that there are still more things we can learn that will help us communicate the world to our special audience.

Through meeting my coauthor in this book, Dr. Ray Hull, I was able to draw on his vast knowledge and experience in the field of communication to begin to understand the process of age-appropriate communication as we describe visual scenes. For example, if you were describing a cityscape, a carnival, or a desert scene to an adult, you might do it one way, but if you were describing that exact same scene to an eight-year-old, you would do it quite differently. Both descriptions might be accurate, but they are not interchangeable. The appropriateness of the communication is determined by the listener, not the speaker.

As a result of the success of the Narrative Television Network and in order to promote the work we do, I began writing books and a syndicated newspaper/magazine column. Writing is a very solitary form of communication in that you don't get any feedback as you are putting your thoughts into words. As you read these words on the page at this moment, it is important to understand that these words came from my thoughts that were dictated months or even years ago to my colleague Dorothy Thompson. These words were edited, formatted into a manuscript, and turned into a book. The books were distributed by publishers to bookstores or online shopping sites where somehow this volume came into your hands so you could be turning these words into your thoughts at this moment. All of this has happened without any feedback being given or received.

When you are talking with someone, based on their responses, expressions, or body language, you begin to understand if your message is being heard, understood, and agreed with. Often, based on these cues, you will change what you are saying or how you are saying it in the middle of a conversation. When you are writing, this is a luxury that is not available. Obviously, you can have colleagues, friends, or editors read your manuscript and provide their feedback, but there is no way for me to know how you are going to react to these words until I write them, and they are printed in their final form as a book.

This book represents my thirty-first title. I have over 10 million books in print in more than two dozen languages, and each of my books, including this one, provides my contact information. Jim@JimStovall.com. 918-627-1000. I have thousands of people from all around the world contact me after reading one or another of my books. Even so, there are millions of people who read words I have written whom I will never hear from. I have no instantaneous or even delayed feedback on whether they understand, enjoy, or even relate to what I am writing.

I have written almost 1,000 weekly syndicated columns under the heading *Winners' Wisdom*. People around the world read these weekly offerings in newspapers, magazines, and online publications. This communication format allows me to more freely share my thoughts and opinions. People may agree or disagree with what I write in my columns, and I welcome this feedback, but I always stress that it is only my opinion, and I am still the world's leading authority on my opinion.

The success of my books and columns gave me the opportunity to communicate in a totally new forum. To date, I have had four of my books turned into movies with several more in production. I am convinced that if Mark Twain, Charles Dickens, or William Shakespeare were alive today, they would not only be writing books, but they would be making movies.

Movies represent one of the greatest forms of cultural communication in our society. While there are millions of people who have read my books, there are many millions more people who will never receive my message through the written word, but they will go to the movies.

While writing is a solitary form of communication, movies are the product of many hundreds of people's creative efforts. My books turn into our movies.

A great movie can communicate thoughts, feelings, and emotions like nothing else, but it requires great writing, acting, and technical production to make this level of communication possible. Great actors, like great writers and speakers, often communicate more by saying less.

I remember working with Brian Dennehy, the esteemed actor, on my first movie entitled *The Ultimate Gift*. The director, who was a bit intimidated by Mr. Dennehy's stardom, was reviewing a certain scene before shooting it. Brian was reading over the script and marking out whole sentences of his dialogue, explaining that those lines weren't necessary.

The director asked, "Mr. Dennehy, how will the young character in the scene understand that your character is frustrated and disgusted with his ignorance?"

Brian gave the director a look communicating that he was frustrated and disgusted with the director's ignorance and didn't say a word.

The director simply said, "Yes, sir, I understand."

Brian Dennehy understands what we all need to remember—that everything we do communicates as much or more than everything we say.

The movies have actually brought together many forms of my own communication including written, verbal, and nonverbal. Ironically, in each of the movies based on my novels, I make a brief cameo appearance playing a limousine driver. While you may think it's absurd, humorous, or even dangerous for a blind person to be the limo driver, I can assure you no one has been injured thus far in the production of any of my scenes within the movies.

I'm often fascinated that through my words and images on a movie screen I can communicate the thoughts and emotions of a limo driver even though it is not anything I've ever done or could do in real life.

The success of the movies based on my own books has given me the opportunity to do countless print, radio, and TV interviews. People often think that the news is an accurate form of communication as it delivers timely facts. In reality, it is not always accurate, and it is rarely complete. It is significant that when a person is called upon to testify in a court of law they swear, under oath, and are subject to criminal penalty to communicate the truth, the whole truth, and nothing but the truth. Communicating a half-truth is not accurate communication. Even if you are communicating accurate facts, if you leave out critical and pertinent elements you will communicate false and misleading information.

So, there I was walking onto the stage to deliver my first speech as a blind person to over 14,000 people in an arena. I thought about all the different forms of communication that I had participated in throughout my career and life. Each of them had played a part in putting me on that stage which was the first of many stages where I have been privileged to speak to millions of people around the world.

I often tell people who are confused about what I do for a living that I am not in the TV business, the movie business, the book business, the column business, or the speech business. I am in the message business. My product and my service is my message, but without the art of communication, my message or any message is worthless.

The greatest thoughts, feelings, and emotions remain dormant, awaiting the spark of communication that can bring them to life in the moment and for all time.

CHAPTER 3

THE ART OF INFLUENCING OUTCOMES OF MEETINGS AND INTERVIEWS

Through our ability to communicate in a thoughtful and articulate manner, we can influence the outcomes of meetings and interviews in positive ways. The following are suggestions to be considered when we find ourselves in particularly stressful situations involving interpersonal communication in those environments.

Meetings

As I prepare for meetings, should I anticipate questions and plan my responses ahead of time?

As we plan for meetings, of course we cannot anticipate all of the questions we might be asked. But, we can always plan ahead to the degree possible. If we are already working in that specific organization, we will usually be aware ahead of time of the topics to be covered in a meeting, and will usually know the people who will be attending. So, we can generally anticipate the tenor of the discussions that will take place. We already know those in attendance who will be the most aggressive and argumentative, and those who will be most complacent and agreeable during discussions. We already possess that important knowledge, so we can plan our responses ahead of time and therefore will not be caught off guard. Take advantage of that pre-knowledge and mentally prepare how you are going to interact and how you are going to respond to questions and comments.

When all seems to be falling apart around me, how do I remain calm?

Stay calm and collected even if you find yourself in a stressful meeting, and particularly if you feel as though you are being overwhelmed with questions. During a rather stressful discussion, for example, we must try our very best to *never* look panicked or bewildered. I tell my audiences that one of the best things they can do to make sure that they are in control of themselves in situations of stress is to take a good course in acting. Becoming a good actress or actor is one of the best things we can do to be sure that *we* are in control of ourselves in situations involving stressful meetings, being confronted by an angry client or one of their family members, or in other situations that for one reason or another have become less than positive.

By being visibly under stress, and therefore losing control of the situation we are in at that moment, we are fodder for others who may desire to be in control. That is a situation we do not want to find ourselves in—ever.

What if I become emotional?

In meetings in which matters are being discussed that are personally, organizationally, or politically close to you, do *not* become emotional! That is where that good course in acting can come in handy. We sometimes need to become a good actor or actress to show grace and serenity rather than negative emotions that are visible to others.

Never get into a shouting match over issues, no matter how close they are to you. If you get into a shouting match, you will only regret it later. It is best to simply and calmly thank the other person for their interest or concern. As stated above, it is critically important that we maintain an air of serenity. We must practice smiling so that our smile does not reflect partially concealed irritation or anger. Our smile and manner, even in times of stress and irritation, should reflect genuineness and calm.

Meetings and Interviews

Is it okay to say, "I don't know"?

During an interview or meeting in which you are responding to a number of tough questions, there is absolutely nothing wrong in saying an honest, "I don't know." Or, "I'm not sure, but I will find out for you." Or, "That's a very good question. Let me think about it for a moment." Those are honest responses to what we may find to be difficult questions.

If we absolutely don't know the answer, then an honest, "I don't know the answer to that" is an appropriate response, as long as it is not said too frequently. If we are simply unsure of the meaning of a question, then it is appropriate to request a restatement in different terms. Never, never say, "I'm so sorry, but I don't know the answer." There is no need to apologize. The "I don't know the answer to that, but I will be pleased to find out what it is" should be said with poise and confidence. Not through an apology.

Or, if we cannot answer a question directly, it is always appropriate to relate it to a similar issue or situation that we feel more confident addressing. Those attending the meeting or interview will frequently congratulate you on developing a creative response to their question! It is always best to appear contemplative or thoughtful, but not puzzled, when searching for an appropriate response. Again, poise is the key here rather than appearing puzzled and distraught.

Interviews

In an interview, what if I am asked too many questions at one time?

In an interview, try to avoid responding simultaneously to multiple sub-questions contained in one comprehensive question. Occasionally interviewers will ask these types of complex questions for two reasons: 1) of course, to test your knowledge, but also 2) to assess your ability to handle stress. Of course it is frustrating when an interviewer states, "I have a question for you. However, it has three parts. Those parts are as follows…"

and the primary comprehensive question and its sub-parts are then asked.

First of all, avoid feeling that you must respond to each question in the exact order that the person who asked the question had them listed for you. That is particularly important if you feel that you can answer one of the sub-questions most easily because you are more familiar with the background and content of an appropriate answer.

It is perfectly acceptable to respond by saying something like, "Thank you for that very comprehensive question. If you will allow me, I will begin by responding to sub-question number two first, and then I will move on to the others." Frequently, by the time you have answered sub-question number two, the one you chose to begin with because you felt you would be able to respond to it best, the person who asked the question may very well thank you for your thorough response, and will want to move on with the interview without requiring responses to the two other sub-questions! Of course, I am sure that you will also be ready to move on!

Should I keep my responses to questions as concise as possible, or are longer answers better?

If you are being interviewed for a new position, or for advancement within your existing organization, it is imperative that you keep your responses to questions concise, and not give more information than was requested. Giving more information than was requested can get us into more difficulty than probably anything else during an interview. As I advise my audiences to remember during oral examinations or interviews, "After you have answered a question from a member of the committee, it is best to keep your mouth shut!" What gets interviewees and students into difficulty is when they continue to talk after answering the question! To them, it somehow seems necessary to keep talking; they may fear that perhaps they have not given adequate information in their initial response to the question. In doing so, they find themselves repeating what they have already said. Even more deadly, they may give information beyond what was asked for that is not accurate, and then realize later that it was truly incorrect!

Should I prepare for interview questions and my responses beforehand?

Before entering an interview, take time to consider various things that might occur during the interview and possible questions that might be asked. Better yet, ask the person who is in charge of the interview what the format will be. By preparing, you will be less likely to be caught off guard. Before entering the interview, consider these key questions:

- What haven't I asked about the job beforehand?
- What haven't I been asked beforehand?
- What might *I* appropriately ask during the interview?
- What *might I* be asked?
- Or, as I said above, ask the person who will be in charge of the interview what types of questions might be asked. That is a perfectly appropriate question.

Develop your potential responses to questions before you arrive at the interview site. Most of all, during the interview try your best to never look flustered—even if you are not sure of an answer to a question! It's best to look poised and interested, as though you are thinking, "That's a very interesting question," rather than frowning and silently thinking, "Why in the world would someone ask me that stupid question?" The reason? Your facial expression and body language will tell the interviewers what you are thinking.

Should I talk about myself during an interview?

At an appropriate time during an interview, be sure to add some positives about *you*. When an interviewer asks the question, "Tell us why you are interested in this position, and what would you bring to it?", at that time, it is appropriate to tell those who are interviewing you about the positives that *you* would bring to the organization.

Even if the question is not asked, take a moment toward the end of the interview to say something like, "I want to share with you why I applied for this position, and what I feel I would bring to it." The interviewers will certainly not pass up the opportunity to hear what you have to say! Importantly during those moments, do not hesitate to share your thoughts on the traits and knowledge that *you* possess that would add strength to their organization. Most of all, don't be bashful!

After the Interview

After the interview, *always* follow up with an email or letter to the chair of the search committee, thanking everyone for the opportunity to meet with them and saying how impressed you were with their facilities, the staff whom you had the opportunity to meet, and that if they have any further questions, you would be happy to respond to them. Never ask about salary! If they are strongly considering offering the position to you, they will share that information. You can then decide if you are truly interested in working there.

If I don't like my current position or my boss, should I tell the interviewers about it?

That's an excellent question. Let me tell you this. When interviewing for a new position, and the interviewers have asked you why you are considering leaving your current place of employment, do not use that important moment to criticize your current boss, nor to complain about your current position no matter how much you would like to! Complaining about your current position or criticizing others who work there tends to reflect negatively on you and your professionalism.

Don't ruin an otherwise positive interview by complaining or criticizing. You can simply say, for example, that you happened to see the advertisement for their open position, and it sounded as though it would be an exciting opportunity! Further, you feel that it fits your knowledge and expertise nicely. That is an excellent response, and may very well be all that you need to say.

CHAPTER 4

THE COMMUNICATION CONNECTION

I have long said to aspiring speakers, businesspeople, and those who read my books and syndicated columns, watch my movies, or hear me speak, "Just because you're talking doesn't mean anyone's listening; and just because they're listening doesn't mean anyone's hearing; and just because they're hearing doesn't mean they're understanding; and just because they're understanding doesn't mean they understand what you intend them to."

For this reason, one of the most often-asked and most absurd questions is, "Do you understand?" This is the basis for much miscommunication in our world. People I deal with on a regular basis, personally and professionally, often assure me, "I explained it thoroughly to everyone, and they said yes when I asked them if they understood."

The "yes" response that these people receive is inconsequential. It means absolutely nothing. The pertinent and proper question after any explanation or discussion that will confirm that true communication has transpired is, "What do you understand?"

My late, great friend, mentor, and colleague Dr. Stephen Covey was fond of saying, "Seek first to understand and then seek to be understood."

Dr. Covey went on to explain that in any discussion or conflict, he wanted to be able to articulate the other person's perspective to their satisfaction before he communicated his own position. Faulty or misleading communication is, most often, worse than no communication at all. Someone who doesn't understand something and knows they don't understand it is in a better position than someone who doesn't understand but thinks they do.

Whenever I speak at a business convention or arena event, I realize most of my audience has never met a blind person, or at least they certainly haven't confronted a blind person who is walking back and forth talking to them on a giant arena stage. I always want to put my audience at ease and get past the fact that I'm blind, so I use humor. Humor is often the most powerful form of communication to diffuse an awkward or uncomfortable situation.

I have found the best way to introduce my audiences to my blindness and set their minds at ease so we can go on to discuss more important issues is to tell them a true story about a real experience I had when giving my first speech after losing my sight.

I had been hired to speak at a convention of 14,000 state government workers in an arena in Los Angeles. I had been slowly losing my sight for years, but this would be my first speech as a totally blind person. My friend and colleague, Kathy Harper, was traveling with me on that trip, and she and I were standing backstage reviewing everything I needed to do to get through the speech.

I was tremendously nervous as I tried to remember whether it was 12 steps or 13 to the front of that stage. I can assure you that can be very critical at a certain point in time. I was also trying to remember where all the potted palm trees were located that some misguided stage production worker had decided would look good in the arena for the convention. If you ever run across the man or woman who repeatedly puts potted palm trees on stages in arenas where a blind guy like me is often giving a speech, would you let that individual know I would like to speak with them because over the last several years, I like to humorously say I've had kind of a close relationship with some of those potted palm trees.

In any event, all of these things were going through my mind standing backstage with Kathy as I was waiting to be introduced.

As a blind person, you become very aware of things around you, and I could tell or at least sense that someone had approached us backstage in that arena and seemed to be standing right next to me. I wasn't sure what was going on, so I asked Kathy, and she explained, "Jim, there's a guy standing right next to you holding up a note in front of your face for you read."

I told Kathy I was very nervous, and I didn't have any time for this, but I inquired, "What does his note say?"

Kathy read the note aloud. "I am deaf. Can you please help me find the front desk?"

Without even thinking about it, I turned to the gentleman and explained, "No, I am blind, and can't help you find the front desk or anything else."

I inquired of Kathy as to what the gentleman was doing at that moment, and she explained, "He's holding the note closer."

I'm embarrassed to admit I explained it to him even louder, and we never did establish any real communication between us even though we had his note, my statements, and Kathy to guide us through the communication.

The form, level, and delivery of the communication must be geared to the recipient and not the person initiating the conversation. It is human nature to want to have everyone understand everything we are thinking as we communicate in the way in which we are most comfortable, but if you don't adjust your communication to fit your audience, it will figuratively and sometimes literally fall on deaf ears.

There is a resort on an island in Mission Bay in San Diego, California, where I speak several times each year. I enjoy the little island, and they have a small cottage where my staff and I stay on each of my visits. At this writing, I have been to that resort more than 30 times and stay for several days on each visit.

The staff at the resort is very attentive, and they are well aware that many people travel across the country and around the world to their resort in order to hear me speak. The resort staff knows that I am blind, and several years ago the manager approached me and told me they wanted to accommodate my blindness and efficiently handle the many phone messages I get during each of my stays. To this end, the manager and his staff had developed a plan.

He explained, "Because you can't see the red light on the phone that we use to alert guests they have a message, we will make a message slip for each of your calls, writing down who called, what message they wanted to leave, and the callback number; then we can have one of the bellmen drive over to your cottage and slide the message slips under your door."

As this well-meaning hospitality professional was explaining this to me, I felt as if I were on the old TV show *Candid Camera*. Apparently, it had never occurred to the resort manager or his staff that, while I appreciated his effort and the gesture, for the same reason I couldn't see the red light on the phone I obviously wouldn't be able to read the message slips that someone slid under my door.

This was not a case of inattentive communication or inaccurate communication. It was a case of the communicators not understanding their audience.

Not only does the form of communication need to be appropriate, but the language used must be understood.

The world we live in is getting smaller every day in terms of how we communicate, who we can reach, and how often we communicate with them. My books have been translated into over two dozen languages, and I have come to understand that a good translation is never literal. Just because my words are put in someone else's language, it does not mean that my thoughts are going to be accurately communicated.

Several years ago, I got a call from China from a young lady who was translating one of my books into Mandarin. I always appreciate these calls from translators around the world who are dedicated enough to their craft to display a commitment toward getting my message correct.

In one of my novels, I had described one of my characters in an awkward and somewhat dangerous situation as having "a tiger by the tail." This is a descriptive phrase that most English-speaking people would at least have some understanding of. Descriptive phrases such as having "a tiger by the tail" can often take the place of pages of descriptions. I could say a feeling is like "being on a first date," and most of us would conjure memories that elicit feelings that are common among us.

The young lady translating my book into Mandarin, however, apparently lives in a part of the world where there are tigers in the wild. People in her area have a respect and appropriate caution relating to tigers and could never imagine anyone grabbing "a tiger by the tail," so when she asked me what I meant by that phrase, I explained it to her to the best of my ability, and she asked if it was like "stacking your milk bottles three high." I was baffled and asked her to explain. She informed me that many people in her area of China live in densely populated, high-rise buildings. Milk is delivered to the residents of her building each day, and the empty bottles are placed outside the door. Apparently if you haven't put your empty bottles out in the hall for several days, the limited amount of space can cause you to have to stack them two levels high. As I understand it, this is fairly common, but if you've been remiss in putting your empty milk bottles out for an extended period of time, you might be tempted to stack them three high.

This, as apparently everyone in her culture understands, is very precarious, uncomfortable, and a behavior that is considered on the edge. It is a feeling much like people where I live might describe as having "a tiger by the tail."

I appreciate having dedicated translators around the world who are more interested in translating my message and meaning instead of just my words. If she had accurately translated my words, the readers of my books in Mandarin throughout parts of China would think my character who had a "tiger by the tail" was insane or suicidal instead of just being uneasy, uncomfortable, or "on the edge."

Language is often limiting and confining but sometimes it's all we have to work with. Our culture has become so global that you don't have to go around the world to run into these kinds of language barriers.

For many years, I worked out of a television studio in Washington, DC to do celebrity interviews, network promos, and promotional videos. I remember getting off the plane at Reagan Airport on one trip and being confronted by a frantic gentleman of Asian descent. After several failed attempts to understand his question, I finally understood him to ask me if I knew the White House. I calmly explained that the White House is the home where the President of the United States lives, and it is located at 1600 Pennsylvania Avenue.

In spite of my logical and thorough explanation, the gentleman seemed even more distressed as he repeatedly seemed to ask about phoning the White House. I explained that I did not know the phone number for the White House switchboard off the top of my head, but if he would call directory assistance, they would give it to him.

He frantically objected, and according to my colleague and assistant traveling with me, pointed emphatically at the ceiling of the airport. My colleague and I were both bewildered when I heard an announcement come over the airport public address system. "Mr. Ming, you have a call on the white housephone."

My assistant quickly showed my new acquaintance, Mr. Ming, where the courtesy phones were located so he could receive his telephone call. As I waited for her to rejoin me, I stood in the concourse of Reagan International Airport and contemplated the fact that, as a best-selling author, highly paid professional speaker, television host, and movie producer, I could find it virtually impossible at times to communicate the most simple answers to the most routine questions from someone who was obviously a highly motivated and intelligent person.

The danger in miscommunications is not the fact that they occur but the fact that we, too often, assume they don't occur. Communication without confirmation is like playing with a loaded gun. Sooner or later, in spite of your best efforts and attentions, you will get shot.

In dealing with human communication, there are a myriad of methods, styles, and techniques that can be used, but there are countless barriers, detours, and pitfalls that can interrupt, distort, and totally derail our communications.

Miscommunication too often doesn't simply result in a humorous encounter that can turn into a funny story to share in the future. Miscommunications, in spite of our best intentions, often result in damaged or destroyed relationships, broken homes, failed marriages, global conflicts, and even wars.

CHAPTER 5

THE ART OF NONVERBAL COMMUNICATION

Nonverbal communication can be more powerful, even more influential than what we say with words. Experts in interpersonal communication have estimated that nonverbal communication constitutes approximately 70 percent of what is involved in communication. In other words, only about 30 percent involves the words that we use.

Other research has postulated that the nonverbal aspects of communication account for as much as 93 percent of what we are communicating to others. That is, approximately 38 percent vocal, 55 percent facial expression, and 7 percent verbal—*what* we say. But, placing the impact of nonverbal communication at 93 percent has now been deemed a little high, and so a safer level is thought to be around 80 percent. Even so, placing the impact of nonverbal communication at 80 percent is still impressive! Subtracting the verbal impact of what we say places the combined effect of our vocal expression, our facial expression, and our body language close to 80 percent. That leaves the impact of the words that we use at only about 20 percent.

The history of nonverbal communication has been traced back to the early Hellenic period, about 400 to 600 years BC. That is the approximate time that is thought to include the study of human discourse as a means of communication and influence. Much before that, however, the nonverbal aspects of communication were undoubtedly an important part of relaying information when *homo sapiens* began engaging in social behavior during prehistoric times. We're speaking here about a form of communication used by wolves and by primates. The nonverbal aspects of communication have been basic to survival since time began! This form of communication was probably basic to the early interactive nature of communication between humans before the verbal aspects of language and communication evolved.

Even Charles Darwin was involved in the study of nonverbal communication. In 1872, he published "The Expression of Emotions in Man and Animals," which discussed the forms of nonverbal communication used and their similarities between humans and other species. He concluded that nonverbal communication was a primary "mode of delivery" and placed verbal communication as simply an extension of the nonverbal form.

So, our body language, our facial expressions, and the way in which we present what we say to others are extremely powerful! We must know how to present ourselves in a positive, constructive, nurturing way—our *manner* of presentation—our manner of presentation of *ourselves*!

Nonverbal communication takes a number of forms, from how you walk into the room where your job interview is to take place, to how we sit when communicating with others, the gestures we use when we are talking, and many others. The following will give you suggestions on how nonverbal communication can impact positively or negatively on our ability to interact communicatively with others.

I have heard of something called, "The two minute rule." What is it?

What we call "the two minute rule" is a critically important part of communication. When we enter a room where a meeting is being held, or enter the room for our interview for a new position, or when we walk to the podium to give a presentation, those in attendance will determine their appraisal of us within the first two minutes of our entering their space. That initial appraisal is difficult to erase. It includes our manner of dress (appropriateness of dress will be discussed in Chapter 11), how we enter a room, our eye contact, how we stand or sit, and our use of gestures when we speak, among other things.

Maintaining poise and calming bodily mannerisms will help to create a comforting atmosphere for those in attendance. If we act nervous when we enter the room, those in attendance at that meeting, interview, or presentation will feel it and probably reflect it back to us. It's contagious. They will be just as nervous as you are, and will probably not enjoy what you have to say.

Charles Spurgeon, one of the greatest communicators of the last century, often told his students, "When you talk about Heaven, let your facial expression reflect joy and excitement. When you talk about hell, your normal facial expression will do!" What he was saying in a rather humorous form is that communication involves far more than just words! It involves how we appear, our poise, and our manner of presentation of our self to those with whom we are communicating. We tend to reflect what we are feeling, and that feeling reflects onto those with whom we are communicating. If we are feeling frustrated and angry, that will reflect onto those listening to us, and they may also tend to feel frustrated and angry along with us. If we are happy to be there and express the joy of interacting with them on our face and in our bodily mannerisms, those who are listening to us will tend to pick up on that joy and feel joyous in return!

Sometimes we need to make a mental adjustment, an attitude change before we enter an environment where communication is to take place. If we're not happy, we need to get happy!

At an interview for a new position, or when entering an auditorium and walking to the podium to deliver a presentation, it is appropriate to be nervous. Being a little nervous can keep us on top of the game. Controlling it is the important part. Nervous and happy, or nervous and genuinely glad to be there, if controlled well, can lead to great things!

Is the distance between me and the person with whom I am speaking important?

It is important to remember that we must maintain an appropriate distance from those with whom we are communicating—not too close, but yet not too far. Thirty inches is just about right—no greater and no less. A while back I was speaking with my seventeen-year-old daughter. I was trying to get what I felt was an important bit of advice across to her. After I completed what I was telling her, I asked her if she understood what I had just said. After a slight pause, she said in all seriousness and with perfect eye contact, "Dad, you are standing in my social space."

Out of all that I had just told her, that was her response. Well, I realized then that I was standing closer to her than my usual distance, but was not aware that I was standing in her "social space." She had learned about the importance of socially acceptable distance in school that day, and she was putting what she had learned into practice! So, I apologized and stepped back at least one step. At that point, I again asked her if she understood what I had just told her. She admitted that she had absolutely no idea, except for the fact that she felt that I was saying something important. The fact that I was standing in her social space took priority over hearing and comprehending anything I had just explained to her.

The above is a wonderful example of how important distance is for effective communication. Too close is bothersome to the one with whom we are communicating. If we are too distant, the listener may feel disenfranchised, and for the opposite reason we begin to lose ground in our communication efforts.

I know that good posture is important, but...

Our posture can reveal or communicate to others what we did not intend to reveal. Our posture reveals what we are feeling. I am thinking here about meetings, interviews, or a friendly conversation in the family room over coffee. For example, while sitting and listening to what another person is telling us, leaning too far forward with shoulders hunched indicates that we have already decided against what is being said. We're bored. We've stopped listening.

Or, leaning too far back in our chair with our hand covering our mouth may indicate hostility toward the speaker's ideas or questioning their logic. We're holding back our remarks by covering our mouth.

I tell my audiences that when we are standing and listening to someone who is speaking to us, stand with feet approximately 18 inches apart. If feet are too close together, it can appear that we are about ready to fall, or have assumed a ballet pose. If our feet are too far apart, it can appear that we are about to attack, fight, or are trying out for the football team. Feet kept about 18 inches apart gives the appearance of a comfortable stance—our feet are not too close and not too far apart. The same stance is important when we are giving a presentation to an audience. It tends to give us an appearance of confidence and that we feel comfortable being there.

In other words, what we are when we communicate with others—how we listen, and importantly how we appear, how we sit, and how we stand when we are communicating—make up the "stuff" of communication. If we overlook any of those, communication may frequently simply not take place.

What do I do with my arms and hands and my legs and feet?

Our arms and hands and legs and feet can also reveal a great deal about how we are feeling in regard to what we are listening to as another person speaks to us. For example, arms folded across the chest, especially while standing, can indicate resistance.

While sitting, playing with fingers and nails can indicate that we are not really listening to the other person. We are simply giving ourselves something to do until the other person finishes talking.

Legs crossing and uncrossing or heels or toes tapping are all negative clues, perhaps that we are nervous or that we are ready to leave!

Do *not* put your hands in your pockets or have them clasped behind your back. Holding them in those positions causes us to appear that we are hiding something or that we are bored. Our hands can appropriately be folded in front of us at the level of or just below our waist. The appearance is that we are listening openly, and we are interested in what is being said.

Don't let your hands dangle at your sides. We tend to slouch when we hold them in that manner, and we take on the appearance of being tired. Most importantly, never look at your watch no matter how much you are tempted to. It is a definite signal that we have stopped communicating, and it is time to leave.

If you find yourself in a situation where shaking hands with others is essential, it is very important that we control our handshake—not limp or overly soft, nor overly firm as to cause pain. A "moist-clingy" handshake can repel people faster than one that is too firm. A handshake that denotes sincerity and genuineness is slightly firm, but not overpowering, and warm. Placing your other hand over the hand of the person with whom you are shaking hands is appropriate on occasion, but can appear too personal to some persons. So use it only when you feel that it is appropriate.

Now, what about my eyes?

Our eye movements are important giveaways to what is going on in our mind. For example, lack of eye contact or frequent glances to one side or the other indicate serious disagreement, disinterest, extreme nervousness, or a thought-provoking "why am I even here!"

Eye contact is a seriously important part of communication on an interpersonal basis. Our eyes give us away. If we are talking to someone of the opposite sex, and as we are talking to that person we are looking intently into their eyes, a sense of intimacy is established that we, or they, may not desire to have established.

If our eyes stray below the other person's chin, we may appear to be looking at areas of the body that will make the person we are speaking with feel uncomfortable—we're not supposed to be looking at those body parts!

I tell my audiences, and we do some practice in this area, that the best area of the face to focus on while speaking to another person is their nose. When I am speaking to an audience, no matter how large or how small, I make eye contact with as many in the audience as I can by concentrating on their nose. By concentrating on the nose, it appears that we are concentrating only on that person, and no one else. We aren't looking into the person's eyes (too intimate). We are concentrating on the person's face, and it is a comfortable location both for you and the person or persons with whom we are speaking.

I have a habit of gesturing a lot while I talk. Are there rules that govern that?

Gestures can be an important part of communication. However, it is also important to be aware of their benefits and limitations. If used properly, the appropriate use of hand and arm gestures can give meaning to communication. But if they are overused, they can detract from what we are saying. They can be a distraction rather than an aide to effective communication.

To illustrate that point, last year I was asked to be a judge at a public-speaking competition at a national convention. The competition is held each year to promote leadership among young adults. The topic that was given the contestants was "The Importance of Underrepresented Young Adults Becoming Leaders in Our Society." Each presentation was to last six minutes. As I listened to each of the contestants, I rated them on various aspects of content and manner of presentation.

At the appointed time, one young woman walked to the front of the room and began her speech. First and foremost I noticed two things as she progressed through her speech. She was speaking, I am quite sure, at a rate of around 200 words per minute, and she was waving her arms wildly in many directions! She was either visibly excited about what she was saying or extremely nervous. When her six minutes were up, I realized that I was exhausted by just listening to her! When it was my turn to give my critique of her presentation, I told her that the primary thing that I learned from her speech was that she was evidently very nervous! I told her in what I hoped to be a constructive manner that her extremely rapid rate of speech and her flailing arms were so distracting that I felt that I missed the content of her presentation. Her words were lost! All I received from her message was that she was apparently very nervous. I was wishing that I had been able to video record her presentation so I could have shown her what she was doing that was so distracting, because she was looking at me in what appeared to be disbelief.

The appropriate use of gestures, then, is not overused so that they become distracting to the listener and avoiding random gestures that have no appropriate meaning and can indicate either a lack of confidence in what we are saying, nervousness, or a lack of control over the situation. Prudent use of gestures is the key; do not use them at all unless they will add to the content of what is being said. In the end, speaking with hands clasped in front of us at a little under waist high is always appropriate.

Have you watched a professional singer on stage? Those who possess the highest level of grace and professional demeanor stand with their hands at their sides and feet around 18 inches apart— no gestures, no movement. In that way, the audience attends primarily to their voice, the words, and the melody of the song being sung. Nothing else is there to distract.

Although many of us are not professional singers, we can achieve that level of grace when we speak. When we achieve what I call *grace* or perhaps *serenity*, we are doing nothing else to detract from what we are saying. All the listeners can attend to are the words we are expressing, the use of our voice, our eye contact, the movements of our head and shoulders, and our manner of presenting our self to them.

On the other hand, as we stand before the audience, our demeanor under control, we *will* be demonstrating a form of nonverbal communication. As I said above, our eye contact, the movements of our head and shoulders as we move them forward toward the audience, and the inflectional characteristics of our voice are all nonverbal forms of communication, and in and of themselves are aspects of gestural and intonational language. By using our voice and non-overt body language, we are demonstrating to the audience that we are speaking to them and to them only—not to the ceiling or the walls or the floor.

CHAPTER 6

THE COMMUNICATION CONVERSATION

As a writer, movie producer, columnist, and professional speaker, I make my living and create my life with words. One truth regarding communication that extends to my personal and professional life is the fact that *who* said something is more important than *what* they said or *how* well they said it.

In the platform speaking profession, there are a handful of very accomplished individuals who have risen to prominence because they have delivered a powerful message with tremendous quality over several decades. These individuals are in the highest demand and command the highest fees with the exception of one other group of speakers. This other group of speakers is made up of celebrities. These are athletes, business icons, politicians, and global thought leaders whose names are household words.

One such individual I worked with is Lance Armstrong. Due to his worldwide prominence as a champion athlete and his public battle with cancer, Lance became one of the highest paid professional speakers of all times, commanding a fee well into six figures. His career went into orbit with no end in sight, but then the controversy came to light about possible substance abuse and rule violations. After the famous or infamous interview with Oprah in which Lance Armstrong admitted to all the allegations and the fact that he had been covering up the situation for many years, his career did not decline, it vanished into thin air.

Lance Armstrong went from being able to pick when, where, and for whom he would speak, being able to virtually name his price, to a point where he couldn't get a speech for no-fee at the local Chamber of Commerce. Ironically, Lance Armstrong's message or the quality of his delivery never changed. The fact that his career crashed and burned was not because of what he said or even how well he said it. It was solely due to the perception or the reality of who he was.

When I started the Narrative Television Network in 1988, I had just lost my sight and was facing the frustration of not being able to access movies, television, and all manner of video programming. With a high-quality and dedicated team, I developed a system that allows the 13 million blind and visually impaired Americans and millions more around the world to access visual media. If you would like to experience how this works, you can check it out at www.NarrativeTV.com.

When NTN first began, the digital revolution in broadcast and cable TV as well as the movie industry had not yet occurred. We could not widely broadcast a program and make our narration soundtrack an option that could be turned on or off at the viewer's discretion. When we launched our service, we only had a few classic movies from the 1940s, '50s, and '60s, and we could only air them on cable TV with the narration intact. This meant I had to convince broadcast stations and cable TV operators that they should carry several hours a week of old movies with an announcer describing the visual elements of the program between the characters' dialogue. This was a tough sell until another challenge required me to find a solution that eventually solved several problems. This solution will forevermore be known at the Narrative Television Network as the Katharine Hepburn Factor.

In addition to not being able to interest most of the people in the broadcast and cable industry in my service, it was pointed out to me that our movies, on average, were too short and did not fit the two-hour format for the blocks of satellite time I had agreed to utilize to deliver NTN programming to TV stations across the country.

The only solution that I could think of to resolve the program length and satellite challenge involved me hosting an interview/talk show with some of the classic film stars who were in the old movies we were narrating as my guests. As improbable as it seems today for a blind guy from Oklahoma with no entertainment industry experience to pursue hosting such a show, that's exactly what we did.

My colleague Kathy Harper, who was legally blind, and I went to the public library to do some research. We were, indeed, the proverbial blind leading the blind. Kathy took her giant magnifying glass which allowed her to read normal print in books, and we wandered up and down the aisles of bookshelves until she spotted a book entitled *Addresses of the Stars*. Fortuitously, that book had the current mailing addresses for most of the classic film stars who were in the movies we were narrating for television.

We went back to our office, which at that time was located in the basement of a condominium building in Tulsa, Oklahoma, and wrote a one-page letter to some of the biggest stars from the Golden Age of movies asking them to be part of my non-existent talk show on my yet-to-launch network. Kathy and I had a brief moment of silence and dropped the letters in the mail.

Approximately 10 days later, we received the first response in the mail. The return address simply said, *Katharine Hepburn, New York City*. My initial thought was, *Even if she turned me down, maybe she signed the note and at least I'll have an autograph.*

When someone in our office opened the letter and read it to me, it simply said, "Dear Mr. Stovall, if you'll call this number...we can discuss the interview." It was, indeed, signed by the grand lady herself, the one-and-only Katharine Hepburn.

I picked up the phone and dialed the number that was read aloud to me, expecting to talk to Katharine Hepburn's secretary, assistant, or manager, and was stunned when Katharine Hepburn answered the phone herself with that iconic Katharine Hepburn voice. I recovered my senses long enough to stammer, "Miss Hepburn, I'm surprised you answer your phone."

She responded in her matter-of-fact tone that I came to love and respect, "Don't you answer your phone? I've always felt when one's phone rings, one should answer it."

I readily agreed with her, and after a brief conversation, we agreed upon a time and place for the interview.

Sitting next to Katharine Hepburn and interviewing her was a life-changing experience for me. Not as much because of what she said or even how well she said it but because of who she was. After we completed the interview, our team flew back to Tulsa and got back to work, but the world had changed because of the aforementioned Katharine Hepburn Factor. Now when I called on broadcast stations or cable television systems, I could mention the movie we would be broadcasting starring Katharine Hepburn with our exclusive interview with Miss Hepburn.

To call it a "game changer" would be an understatement. Some of the other stars I had requested interviews with, and their management, began contacting me. They were skeptical and non-committal until I told them about our upcoming movie and the interview with Katharine Hepburn.

Using the magic words "Katharine Hepburn" was like turning on the light in a dark room. Night became day, and in the coming weeks and months, I interviewed Frank Sinatra, Jimmy Stewart, Michael Douglas, and a myriad of other luminaries that launched the Narrative Television Network.

Today, NTN programming is available around the world, on demand, for many primetime TV shows and first-run movies. It has changed the world for millions of blind and visually impaired people and their families, but it would have been a different story without the help of one grand old lady who opened all the doors, not because of what was said or how well it was said, but because of who said it.

While most of us will never be able to approach the impact that a Katharine Hepburn could have, we do have the ability to increase our credibility and become both knowledgeable and recognizable for the thoughts we express and the words we use.

I am a big believer of the concept I call *putting yourself in the story*. If I read a book, hear a speech, or catch an item in the news that I want to use in a book, a speech, a column, or just in routine conversation, I find it to be extremely valuable when I can have a connection to that source.

If I read a book that I want to refer to through one of my various communication channels in the future, I will call or write to the author with a question or comment. These contacts often result in ongoing dialogue or even friendships. I make the same types of connections with speakers I hear or newsmakers who are in the current media.

By doing this, I can create context and credibility that I would otherwise not have. The difference between saying, "I read where Donald Trump said…" or "Colin Powell expressed…" or "Margaret Thatcher announced…" and "Donald Trump told me…," "Colin Powell shared with me…," or "Margaret Thatcher dropped me a note saying…" is immense. Now I can almost hear the skeptics reading this saying, "Well that's great if you're a best-selling author, Emmy Award winner, or movie producer, but what about the rest of us?"

Please remember, I started this pursuit when I was an unknown blind guy from Oklahoma trying to figure out how to get into the movie, television, and publishing industries. The age-old phrase applies, "If I can do this, anyone can do this."

While I maintain that "who said it" is more important than "how they said it" or "what they said," it is vital that you and I control the environment and the words we use to communicate. Whether it's a movie, a TV interview, or an arena speech, rarely does everything go the way you want it to.

I remember giving a speech for a corporate event in Memphis, Tennessee. I remember it was a round amphitheater venue, and it had a semicircle stage that created some special challenges for me and required my normal walkthrough to memorize the stage to be considerably longer and more difficult than normal. They were having challenges with the sound system, and the buses were delayed getting many of the attendees to the site. Suffice it to say, by the time they were ready for me to go onstage and give my speech, I felt as if I had already run a marathon.

People often wonder how I, as a blind person, connect with my audience and receive feedback from them as I am speaking when most speakers just look out into their audience and can tell if the people are relating to what they're saying and are resonating with their message. Every audience has a different feel and emotion. You can hear telltale sounds and almost feel the emotion in the atmosphere.

On that particular day in Memphis, in spite of working on a round stage, having technical problems during the sound check, and having a long and stressful wait before the event began, my speech was going well, and I could feel the audience relating to me both intellectually and emotionally. Then in an instant, the atmosphere in the amphitheater changed. I wasn't sure what had happened, so I employed one of the most difficult techniques a platform speaker uses, and I simply paused.

Whether you're speaking to a thousand people or one person, a pause can be very awkward, but it is often an effective communication technique. As I paused on that stage in Memphis for what seemed like two minutes, and in reality was not more than a few seconds, I faintly heard technicians whispering backstage, and I instantly came to the realization that all the lights in the entire building had gone out. As a blind person, it didn't matter to me, but I realized my audience would be disrupted, uncomfortable, and prone to panic.

I said the first thing that came to my mind. "Ladies and gentlemen, welcome to my world."

Laughter resounded throughout the amphitheater, and thunderous applause erupted. I don't think they were ever sure if I did it on purpose or if the electrical service to the building had been interrupted.

A few moments later, the lights came back on. I finished my speech, and the crowd blessed me with a thunderous standing ovation. I have given hundreds of speeches since that one in Memphis, but I still hear from people who were in that amphitheater that day. A potential disaster turned into a memorable milestone because of a brief pause and one line that communicated a sense of well-being, humor, and perspective to my audience.

While you don't want to court problems when you're communicating, you do want to realize that challenges always arise, and how you deal with them can communicate more than your words or your message.

Because of my work on the Narrative Television Network and the fact that we received an Emmy Award for our first season on national television, I was invited to be on *Good Morning America.* It was a great opportunity for me, NTN, and the audience we serve as I would be doing a four-minute, sit-down interview with Charlie Gibson and then ABC would run a brief clip of one of our narrated movies. Four minutes may not seem like a lot of time in your daily routine, but on network TV it is a gold mine.

We flew to New York City, got up in the middle of the night to get to ABC studios a couple of hours before *Good Morning America* went on the air live. After they put me through the process of having makeup smeared all over my face, I was escorted to the Green Room where I was to wait until it was my turn to be on the show. I met several other businesspeople and politicians who were also going to be guests on that day's program. We chatted nervously awaiting our turn on *Good Morning America.*

After what seemed like I had waited several days, they finally came to get me and escort me to the GMA set. I shook hands with Charlie Gibson, and the floor director let me know we were in a two-and-a-half-minute commercial break and then they would go to my live interview with Charlie Gibson.

Mr. Gibson made me feel very comfortable, and we chatted amiably until a disembodied voice from a sound booth somewhere in the facility declared, "One minute to air." Charlie Gibson and I fell silent, straightened our ties, and prepared for our conversation on live television.

As they were giving Mr. Gibson the 10-second countdown, the disembodied voice interrupted, announcing, "Charlie, we're cutting live to DC for the president."

Everything fell silent in the ABC studio in New York where I sat on the sofa with Charlie Gibson anticipating my big break on national TV. I was afraid to speak, not knowing whether we were on the air or not, when Charlie Gibson stood up and said, "Jim, that's all for now. There won't be any interviews today."

This was devastating as we had spent weeks contacting all of the broadcast stations, cable television outlets, and sponsors we were pursuing to let them know I was going to be on *Good Morning America* discussing the Narrative Television Network.

As I returned to the Green Room, I could hear the president's voice coming through the speakers describing something about our policy as a response to the situation in the Middle East. The other would-be guests who were also in the Green Room awaiting their moment in the spotlight ranted, raved, and complained about the unfairness of the situation. Several of them were rude and abrupt with the *Good Morning America* staff, and eventually they all stomped out of the Green Room and left the ABC studio.

I just sat there, considering how I might recover from the embarrassment of announcing to everyone in the industry that I was going to be on *Good Morning America* that day, and it didn't happen. Then someone sat down next to me, and that familiar voice of Charlie Gibson said, "I appreciate your patience and good attitude about this. Can you stay until tomorrow and do six minutes with me?"

He went on to explain that because they had the film clip of an NTN movie they could show, they would use it as the promo on all of the network programming throughout the day to promote tomorrow's show. My four-minute career break had just turned into a six-minute windfall.

The people at ABC were patient, and Charlie Gibson was extremely accommodating, but I don't feel it would have happened if I had argued and complained like the other guests. Once again, my communications were rewarded, not because of what I said, but because of what I didn't say.

There are environmental factors that impact our communications. We can't ignore them, and we have to realize that we will be rewarded or penalized based on how we handle them.

When I started doing regular talk shows for the Narrative Television Network, we began working out of a studio in Dallas very near the airport. This particular studio did not have adequate soundproofing, so often you could hear the jets taking off and landing. Our floor director actually kept a printout on hand of the flight schedules, but even with our best efforts, occasionally I had to redo a segment due to the noise from the airliners.

This was okay when it was just me alone on the set introducing a movie or promoting next week's show, but when I had a prominent guest, I couldn't ask them to redo an entire segment; but I couldn't simply ignore the noise in the background.

I remember interviewing the esteemed actor Douglas Fairbanks, Jr., and right in the middle of one of his great reminiscences about his film career, a jet flew over. Being an on-camera professional for over half a century, Mr. Fairbanks continued as if nothing had happened. But when he finished his remarks, I felt I needed to say something because I knew that sound would be heard on the air when we broadcast the show; so I simply turned to Mr. Fairbanks and said, "Thank you for sharing that, and this segment is obviously brought to us by Southwest Airlines."

Mr. Fairbanks chuckled and quipped, "They're obviously a fine organization and seem to be running on time today."

We went on with the interview, and it was a great success.

That next week, we sent that portion of my conversation with Douglas Fairbanks, Jr. to the ad people at Southwest Airlines, and they loved it. I believe it had a lot to do with the great sponsorship relationship we enjoyed with Southwest Airlines for several years.

One of the most difficult communication challenges occurs when you are being translated live while speaking to an audience that is hearing your words processed through a language translator. I remember speaking to a group in Mexico, and the translator and I were having some challenges getting into the back-and-forth flow of the exchange.

I felt the audience became impatient and nervous, so I paused, walked up to the edge of the stage, and said, "Ladies and gentlemen, I would like to introduce you to my colleague and a tremendous professional," and I introduced my interpreter. The audience applauded politely, and I continued, "If anything I say is funny, emotional, or impactful, it came from me. If it is not funny, emotional, or impactful, just understand that I got a bad translation."

The audience erupted with laughter, but more importantly, the translator and I relaxed and got into a comfortable flow that helped us through the rest of the evening.

As my late, great friend and mentor, John Wooden, often told me, "We can't always choose what happens to us, but we can always choose what we're going to do about it."

Sometimes, the people with whom you are communicating or the prevailing conditions will make the process difficult, but you can still choose to keep the communication on the highest level possible.

CHAPTER 7

THE ART OF
CONSTRUCTIVE LISTENING

Smith and Williamson call listening a "process."[1] According to those authors, too many times we tend to make listening a "role," something that is required of us, rather than something that we do because we need to and even want to because we care about the one who is speaking or are interested in what is being said. Listening involves hearing, attending, understanding, and remembering what was said.[2] Good listening is "active listening." We actually participate in the *process* of communication when we become an active listener.

I have a hard time being what I consider to be a good listener.
But I'm not sure I know what being a good listener involves!

According to Wilson, Hantz, and Hanna, there are areas that we must concentrate on in order to become what is considered to be a good listener.[3] Those involve:

1. Giving the speaker (the one we are listening to) cues that we are listening. Those involve both verbal and nonverbal cues which can mean being empathetic but not demeaning by implying, "You poor thing!" if the person with whom we are communicating is relaying a sad occurrence in her or his life.

2. No side glances. That's a dead giveaway that we are not really interested in what the person is saying to us.

3. Showing the person who is sharing with us that we are listening carefully to what is being said by maintaining good eye contact, and showing that we are emotionally engaging in what is being said through our body language.

4. Showing that we are listening by occasional nods, an occasional "yes," and brief summaries of what they have said in order to assure that we understand. For example, we might say, "Let me make sure I understand what you are saying," and then give the brief summary of what you think you heard.

5. Offering verbal expressions of feeling if the person is externalizing their thoughts. For example, "That must have made you very angry."

6. Maintaining good eye contact. As I stated in a previous chapter, maintaining good eye contact is an important component in the process of communication. By concentrating on the speaker's nose rather than their eyes or other body parts, it appears that we are focusing our attention directly on that person without giving an appearance of being too intimate.

What are other things I should do in developing good listening skills?

1. If the person you are listening to asks your opinion about a matter that is a concern, answer directly and honestly. Don't hedge or try to circumvent your response. The person who is talking to you is looking for your opinion. Don't be afraid to give it!

2. Don't deny the reality of the concern that is being expressed by saying, "Oh...you're making too much out of it," or "You worry too much!" It is best to simply listen carefully and constructively and allow the person to express her or himself.

3. When listening, and when asked your opinion about what is being expressed, try diligently to see things from the other person's point of view. Never try to stress *your* point of view over theirs, in that way negating their opinion in order to indicate that your opinion is correct and theirs is not.

4. When someone who is close to you is expressing their thoughts or concerns, do *not* interject your opinions

before the other person has finished talking. Even though you feel that you have the solution, interrupting is both inappropriate and disrespectful. It shows that you really didn't want to hear the person's concerns and wanted to solve it quickly so you could go on with whatever you were previously doing. I feel that men are guilty of this more frequently than women.

I have heard that good listening is a sign of a good leader. What does that mean?

Listening is a skill—a skill that is developed over time by those who desire to become excellent communicators. It is true that people appreciate good listeners more than good talkers. Those who are good leaders in any organization are inevitably also considered to be the best listeners. They know when to listen and when to express themselves. In turn, they expect the person or persons to whom they are talking to likewise be good listeners. It is not simply desired; it is expected. A good leader, then, knows when to talk and when to listen.

People are generally not born with good listening skills. Children will sometimes cause parents to feel as though they are "talking to a door" because children have the ability to appear to be listening, but when asked "What did I just say?" it becomes apparent that they were not paying a bit of attention. Adults often engage in the same poor listening habits. That is because they were never taught to be a good listener.

Good listening skills include a package of habits that can be developed. According to the book *Attributes of Good Listening*, good listening requires practice similar to good writing or good speaking. The authors state further that poor listening habits are very common. That is truly an understatement!

Poor listening habits become clearly evident in university teaching. After information is given clearly in class, a portion of the students will inevitably raise their hand just before an examination and ask for a definition of a term that was just given in the previous class period. A few moments later, another student will raise their hand and ask the same question!

So, what are the attributes of good listening?

According to "The Public Speaker: How to Improve Listening Skills," there are three important steps to effective listening skills.[4] Those include:

1. **Tune In**. Tuning in is the very first step in achieving any level of effective listening. We must be both physically and mentally prepared to "tune in." The author states that that means aligning her body with the other person and maintaining eye contact—giving the speaker her undivided attention.

    It also means turning off any mind chatter—erasing anything else you are thinking about. Marshall also advises suspending judgment regarding what the speaker is saying before the speaker has finished. It is important to wait until the other person finishes speaking before creating an opinion and a response.

    Furthermore, it is important to show the person who is speaking that you are truly listening. Lean toward the person who is speaking, nod your head occasionally. We are then not just listening. We are encouraging the one who is speaking.

2. **Internally translate and interpret what we hear**. We determine the meaning of what is being said based on our own experiences, so it is important that we ask questions to confirm our understanding.

   We also must pay attention to the nonverbal aspects of what is being said, not just the words that are being spoken. Those include tone of voice and any gestures that are being used. Does the conversation partner appear excited, sad, or confused?

3. **We must at all costs work to avoid miscommunication**. By confirming our understanding by paraphrasing or rewording what we heard, we can avoid misunderstanding what was said. By asking, "Did you mean…?" or "Did I understand you to say…?" we can clarify the meaning and intent of what was said.

Improving listening skills is not difficult. By following the three steps above, we can develop better insight into what people are really saying to us and thus become better listeners.

What are things that can keep me from being a good listener?

According to "Listening Skills: Why You Need to Be an Active Listener," there are, of course, barriers to effective listening.[5] Those can include:

1. **Our own biases and prejudices**. Those can become a roadblock to listening. If we have already decided that we do not like or respect the one who is speaking, then listening constructively and with an open mind becomes almost impossible. Recognizing our biases is important. It gives us a basis for working to get over them.

2. **An inability to understand the speaker because of a foreign dialect**. In this instance, if you want to hear and understand what the speaker is saying, simply request that she or he speak slower, that you are having difficulty understanding what they are saying. If we request that change constructively and positively, the speaker will probably comply, or at least try.

3. **An inability to hear because of background noise**. If background noise is a problem, ask the person with whom you are speaking to move to a quieter place for a while so you can hear with greater clarity. Noise is a problem in many environments and can result in a breakdown in communication.

4. **Worry or fear that preoccupies our thoughts**. If that is the reason for a "listening breakdown," then we may want to wait until another time to carry on our conversation.

5. **A short attention span**. A shortened attention span can be caused by a number of factors including concerns that are occupying the mind of the listener,

environmental distractions, having difficulty seeing the speaker because of physical barriers, time pressures, or simply being tired. If they cannot be corrected immediately, then it is appropriate for the conversation to be delayed until they can be.

Notes

1. Dennis R. Smith and L. Keith Williamson, *Interpersonal Communication: Roles, Rules, Strategies, and Games* (Dubuque, IA: W.C. Brown, 1991).

2. Gerald L. Wilson, Alan M. Hantz, and Michael S. Hanna, *Interpersonal Growth through Communication* (Dubuque, IA: Wm. C. Brown Publishers, 1989).

3. Ibid.

4. Lisa B. Marshall, *Smart Talk* (New York: St. Martin's Press, 2013).

5. Dawn Rosenberg McKay, "Listening Skills: Why You Need to Be an Active Listener," About Careers, Barriers to Listening, accessed August 17, 2015, http://careerplanning.about.com/cs/miscskills/a/listening_skill.htm.

CHAPTER 8

COMMUNICATION IMAGES AND ILLUSIONS

Often, we think our words are all we have to communicate our message and meaning. Even in a face-to-face conversation, there is much more to the communication process than simply the words we use. There is tone, volume, expression, and body language.

Oftentimes, how we say something is more important than what we say. A simple statement such as, "You look great today," can be a sincere compliment, a shallow comment, a humorous retort, a sarcastic barb, or even a cutting insult. Our tone, inflection, and expression can make all the difference.

As we become more dependent upon our digital devices to communicate, it is increasingly imperative that we communicate not only our words and our message but include our true meaning. It is amazing how much time I spend in my office with other staff members gathered around the computer screen trying to determine what someone meant by the words they typed in an email or blog post.

There are communication shortcuts that involve shared images, impressions, or experiences. If I say, "September 11," or "the 1980 U.S. hockey team," or "Lance Armstrong," we all have shared impressions, images, and memories. There are people's names that elicit an entire scenario that we can use to illustrate our point. We can take a lot of time and energy to describe a person, or we can compare them to Mother Teresa, Bernie Madoff, Osama bin Laden, Richard Nixon, Winston Churchill, or Michael Jordan. Each of these individuals conveys universal images, impressions, and messages. Their actions and their lives have come to stand for something we all recognize.

Only in the last few generations have human beings been able to communicate using shared images. This is greatly due to the impact of movies, television, and the Internet. I remain convinced that if William Shakespeare, Mark Twain, or F. Scott Fitzgerald were alive today, in addition to their writing, they would be turning their words into stories that would end up on movie or television screens around the world.

In the context of human history, it is only very recently that people around the world have shared impressions and images in their minds of Mount Everest, the Oval Office, the Vatican, and the pyramids. In times gone by, to communicate about any of these places, you would first have to expend a great deal of energy, effort, and time to describe a place or setting that the other person had no context or image to draw upon.

Movies have not only provided imagery. They have created a universal vernacular. Think of all the phrases such as "Go ahead. Make my day," "Life is like a box of chocolates," or "I'm going to make him an offer he can't refuse," and countless others. These phrases are constantly repeated by people around the world who are not just using the words but are sharing the images, the emotion, and the story from which the phrase originated.

In times gone by, discussing the news, a cultural event, or an issue of the day involved first telling the other person what happened, when it happened, and how it happened. Today, when you talk with a friend, colleague, or even a stranger about a news item, a sporting event, or a TV program from the previous night, it is assumed that they saw the same thing you saw or at least have been made aware of it by someone else. These assumptions can be very useful as we communicate, but we must be cautious using them in global terms with people around the world from different cultures, backgrounds, and experiences.

As an American, if I discuss issues in the Middle East, the Japanese economy, or the growing economy in India with people from another culture, I may assume we have a shared image and interest, and that may or may not be the case. Seeking common ground is a powerful communication tool, but assuming we are on common ground when we may not be can create miscommunication, confusion, and conflict.

There are two sides to every story. In the United States, the most painful and divisive historical event may be the Civil War. It pitted brother against brother, friend against friend, and family against family for a number of complex reasons and motives. To this day, 150 years after the war, there are still people on both sides of the argument. People north of the Mason-Dixon Line might be surprised to know there are people in the South who refer to the conflict as "the war of northern aggression."

I remember the emotional and impactful experience of visiting the *Arizona* memorial in Pearl Harbor. The ship still lies on the bottom of the harbor with part of the hull protruding just as it did the day it sank in 1941. Visitors to the memorial reach the site on ferry boats that carry 40 or 50 passengers at a time to and from the platform built on the hull of the warship. The day I visited the memorial, the majority of the people on the boat that shuttled my family and me to the site were Japanese tourists. They came to the experience culturally from a different place, but we all shared an emotional experience.

After my visit to Pearl Harbor, I did some reading and independent study on why the Japanese attacked Pearl Harbor and gained a different perspective than I had held from just learning about World War II in my grade school, high school, and college history courses. Perspective is everything in communication and conversation.

It has long been an unwritten rule of conversation that unless you know someone extremely well, you should avoid topics involving sex, religion, and politics. It's not that there's a lack of things to discuss surrounding those topics, it's the fact that everyone may have differing, strongly held beliefs regarding those issues.

The morning after the Super Bowl, it is understood that most people either watched the game or are aware of the outcome, but this doesn't mean you can assume common ground and just blurt out, "Wasn't that a great game?" or "What a disappointing finish in the Super Bowl." Unless or until you know the other person's loyalties, you can't know how to approach the topic.

There are certain types of communication that are so powerful and persuasive they can create common and lasting images and impressions for virtually all of us. Two of the most powerful orators of all times lived during the same era and were on opposite sides of the global conflict in World War II. Winston Churchill and Adolf Hitler each had the ability to elicit the strongest emotion and galvanize the masses to action simply through the force and eloquence of their words.

As a young platform speaker, I was asked to give a presentation at a local church in my town. I don't often speak in churches as I leave matters of doctrine, religion, and faith to theologians who have dedicated their lives to that important realm; however, from time to time I receive an invitation to give one of my standard speeches in a faith-based setting, and I accept those invitations. I will never forget one such occasion. The elderly minister had heard me speak at a business event and was adamant that I should come and speak to his congregation. I got there early, which is my habit being a blind person and needing considerable time to familiarize myself with the stage and surroundings. This afforded me almost an hour to talk to this minister whom I learned had just celebrated his 90th birthday. He was complimenting me on the speech I had given for the business group, and I was telling him of my admiration for clergy like him who delivered a different message to the same congregation week after week.

As we talked further, I learned we shared similar admiration for many authors, historical figures, and speakers. I was amazed to learn that he had been a speech writer for Winston Churchill and had authored the words that became known as the "Iron Curtain" speech so powerfully delivered by Churchill. I told the minister I collect the recordings of many great speeches and had re-listened to the Iron Curtain speech within the past month or so. I told him I thought Churchill may have been the second-best speaker I had ever heard. The wise old minister chuckled and asked, "Who do you feel is the best speaker you ever heard?"

I'm sure I paused and stammered a bit before I could reply, "Well, if you consider delivery and impact and overlook content, I would have to say Adolf Hitler gave the best speech I ever heard."

I wasn't sure what kind of reaction to expect from the minister but was amazed and a bit confused when he laughed heartily and then explained, "Your impression of Mr. Hitler's speaking ability was shared by Sir Winston."

Ironically, these two monumental speakers who faced each other across the English Channel in a global conflict that changed history could disagree on every point of politics, procedure, and human rights but still respect one another's abilities to communicate.

My late, great mentor, colleague, and friend, Paul Harvey, faithfully delivered the news of the day to several generations of Americans. Mr. Harvey was respected by the majority of his colleagues and people he served throughout his life for being objective, but Mr. Harvey told me on several occasions that everyone has a bias, and many times the most objective thing you can do when communicating is to reveal your own bias. Mr. Harvey explained that beyond how he delivered the news of what he said was the dominant matter of which stories he determined to present in his newscast.

He said, "Often, the greatest bias is revealed not by how a story is reported but by the fact that it's not reported at all." What you don't say can communicate volumes. Mr. Harvey also taught me that admitting I don't know something is far better than saying something and then having to admit later I was wrong.

The news takes on a power of its own because of its frequency, intensity, and dominance. It's easy to get caught up in the fury of the headlines and lose perspective on reality. News stories are not common, everyday, average reality. They are unusual, obscure occurrences, which is what makes them the news. You will never read headlines saying, "Millions of people went to work today, did a great job, cared for their families, respected their neighbors, and made life around them better for everyone." But that's the reality to a much greater extent than the headlines you do read each day.

One of Hitler's most-often repeated quotes is, "If you tell a lie long enough and loud enough, it becomes the truth."

In these cases, the event or happening isn't the story. The story becomes the story. In our society today, the media has created people who are famous for nothing more than simply being famous. No one is quite sure why these individuals came to prominence, but through the media, we seem to care where they go, what they do, who they're with, and what they wear. The media likes to create heroes and loves to destroy them. Whether it's Richard Nixon, Monica Lewinsky, or Lance Armstrong, bringing the famous and prominent to their knees seems to be our favorite contact sport.

My colleague and mentor Coach John Wooden was fond of telling his players, "You will be known for a lifetime of great things you do or one lapse in judgment."

Too often, we select political candidates, job applicants, or even friends not as much for who they are or what they stand for as much as one statement they did or didn't say. I can think of several presidential candidates who would have probably ascended to becoming the most powerful person on earth except for one brief misstatement they made. We live in a sound-bite world, and therefore, every phrase, comment, and statement must be considered carefully because they won't let you take it back or even explain it away.

It was William Shakespeare who helped us all understand that "A rose by any other name would smell as sweet." In this famous passage, Shakespeare taught us that the word *rose* holds no power or sweetness or beauty. It is the image of the actual rose itself that conveys beauty and wonder.

Words only have the power and meaning we give them. There are certain derogatory terms, profanities, and racial slurs that most of us know better than to utter to anyone; however, what we don't say may be more powerful than what we do say. These words are given far too much power and import because we don't dare to even say them. In the wonderful *Harry Potter* books, there was a fictional character who was so evil and so frightening that the characters in the stories would not even mention the name as if the sound alone carried some power or force.

Through my experience in founding and running the Narrative Television Network, I had the opportunity to interview many great stars and entertainers. Among the greatest of these was Frank Sinatra. I got to spend 20 or 30 minutes with Mr. Sinatra in his hotel suite before he did a concert in Dallas with the symphony orchestra. Mr. Sinatra was everything I hoped he would be, and interviewing him was one of the high points in my career.

Several months after filming that interview, my wife and I were in Las Vegas for one of my speaking engagements, and I heard that Frank Sinatra was opening the ballroom at the brand new MGM Grand Hotel. Through some pulled strings and a diligent, dedicated concierge, we got tickets for the opening night. I didn't realize until we arrived at the concert that Don Rickles was going to open the show for Mr. Sinatra. Rickles burst onto the stage and did 45 minutes of his non-stop, rapid-fire, politically incorrect, insulting comedy which delighted and entertained the audience.

Just before he left the stage, Don Rickles paused and became very serious for just a few moments. He said, "I have made my living for many years making fun of us all. As a Jew, myself, I understand what hatred and prejudice can mean, but as long as we're laughing at one another, we're not hating, killing, or destroying."

I have learned much about communication from great educators and scholars, including my coauthor Dr. Ray Hull, but one of the greatest lessons in communication may have been given to me by Don Rickles in his opening act in Las Vegas. Ancient wisdom has told us that laughter is good medicine, and our world is, indeed, in desperate need of a prescription.

Across language and culture, we must find common ground in order to communicate. Sometimes, common ground does not exist so we must come to the agreement that we have a different perspective from others with whom we are communicating.

I'm in the habit of getting up very early each morning. Part of my ritual involves listening to the financial news from Asia on the satellite radio followed by my local news and then the sports updates. I remember a morning when all three satellite radio outlets were reporting on an image that had appeared overnight on the Internet. The image was apparently a photograph of a simple dress. It had gone viral on the web around the world because some people swore the dress was blue and black while others were adamant it was gold and white.

When I got to the office, I had one of my colleagues pull it up on her computer, and she informed me definitively the dress was white and gold. Then I called a couple of other colleagues into her office and asked them to look at the same image on the same computer screen, and they vigorously asserted that the dress was black and blue. No amount of argument, debate, or discussion would resolve the issue. As a blind person, myself, I was fascinated with this controversy in my own office and, literally, around the world over one simple dress.

Sometimes, the only communication tool at our disposal is to simply agree to disagree. People on opposite sides of the dress-color issue could never discuss the style, fabric, or fashion elements of the dress much less who's wearing it, where they're going, and what they are doing as long as they are arguing about the color. Only when they would agree to disagree could they move forward and find other common ground to continue the communication.

Oftentimes, the need to agree to disagree goes far beyond a simple dress and impacts issues of life and death. In one of my novels entitled *Keeper of the Flame*, I wrote about a mythical island inhabited by two tribes of natives. On one side of the island, the natives worshiped the sunrise. They were grateful for the warmth and light it gave which signaled a new day. On the opposite side of the island, the tribe worshiped the sunset as they gave thanks for everything that had happened that day and prepared for a restful night.

The two sides of the island were separated by a giant, almost insurmountable mountain, so the two tribes had very little interaction, and when they did encounter one another, it was often hostile and violent. The two tribes lived on the same island and were similar in every way except for their individual perspectives on the sunrise versus the sunset. They could not even come together in the common ground of agreeing to disagree until they had a mountaintop experience that gave them each a practical understanding of the other's perspective.

Much of the conflict, strife, and war that our world encounters comes more from diverse perspectives than actual disagreement. Doctor Covey's wisdom stating, "Seek first to understand and only then seek to be understood," can serve us all well and make the world a better place.

CHAPTER 9

THE ART OF SPEAKING BEFORE AN AUDIENCE

Public speaking should be considered, as it truly is, an art form, or rather a performing art. If we intend to engage in it, we must prepare to perform. I do not mean to perform recklessly or to perform as a "showoff" or to "stage act." Rather, I mean that if we know that at some time we will be called upon to speak before an audience, it is imperative that we be well prepared, that we learn about the elements that help us to be the best public speaker we can possibly be. Before acting on stage, actors prepare. They attend classes on the art of stage acting, they observe skilled actors to gain knowledge of their techniques on stage—of what makes them great. At the least, those who plan to speak before audiences, or know that they will be asked to do so, should prepare to the degree possible by finding out what will bring them their share of "stardom" when they are asked to walk onto a stage, be handed a microphone, and to "say a few words"!

I find it interesting that among the poorest public speakers I have the misfortune to experience are those who I hear speak at state and national conferences and conventions. I would think that if they are professionals in their field, and are speaking on stage before an audience to tell us of the results of their research or their opinions on a specific subject, they would speak in such a way that we would not have to struggle to hear and understand what they are saying. Or, at a minimum, we would not have to struggle to stay awake!

What are the over-arching problems? They are, among others, 1) the presenter is generally speaking so rapidly that the listener cannot keep up with what is being said; 2) the presenter does not seem to know how to use a microphone efficiently, or at least properly; 3) the presenter does not articulate well enough to be easily understood, or possesses a heavy dialect that interferes with speech intelligibility; or 4) the speaker paces back and forth across the stage so frequently that the audience spends more time locating the speaker than listening to what is being said. The list can go on and on.

This chapter will address difficulties that those who speak before audiences of any size frequently seem to demonstrate. I am referring here to audiences ranging in size from that of a civic organization, at which a speaker has been invited to present a fifteen-minute speech on an upcoming election, to that of a large convention where the audience is in the thousands. Whether the audience is large or small, the demands on the speaker are the same, and the rigor of preparation should be considered equally important.

This chapter will provide you with information on public speaking as a performing art, so that the next time you are asked to speak on stage before an audience, you will not exhibit the difficulties that others seem to demonstrate so frequently.

Why am I so afraid to speak before an audience?

Speaking before an audience is one of the most common fears that people experience. People dread it! Their heart pounds, their palms sweat, their knees become weak, their pupils dilate, and they feel a true sense of dread. There have been a number of studies on the topic of fear that have asked the question, "What is your greatest fear?" Inevitably ranked above fear of heights, illnesses, drowning, falling, death, flying, and other common aspects of life that can cause fear, speaking in front of an audience is usually ranked at or near the top of the list.

So, if you are afraid of speaking in public, you are definitely not alone! It is, for one reason or another, one of the most common fears among humans. I have seen people who I felt should have no fear when standing before an audience become nearly zombie-like as they stand on stage. I remember one beautiful young woman—whom I had admired from afar because of her grace, her stature, and even her ability to walk into a room and silence it simply because of her presence—breaking into tears as she stood before a small audience of peers. I was stunned to see her leave the stage a trembling, sobbing shell of what I had earlier imagined her to be.

I grew up a severe stutterer, and I know full well the fears that come with the task of speaking before an audience. I was terribly embarrassed one day when my high-school public-speaking teacher made each of us stand by our desk and introduce ourselves to the rest of the class. I stood next to my desk and found that I could not even say my name because of my stuttering blocks; all that I could emit from my mouth was "ma—ma—ma—ma—ma—" as I attempted to say, "My name is…." I quickly sat down with my face covered by my hands in order to hide my embarrassment. I knew fear, embarrassment, and ridicule over and over again during my younger years. In order to overcome the stuttering, I decided to enter every opportunity to speak in front of audiences. I auditioned for plays, I entered speaking contests, I became so fluent that I won the state intercollegiate oratory competition my senior year in college!

By overcoming my stuttering and the resulting fear of speaking and somehow becoming a sought-after public speaker, I have come to a point in my life that I truly enjoy getting up before an audience and attempting to "wow them" with what I have to say. In order to break the ice with the audience and give me my sense of balance as I stand on stage, I usually say, "I'm truly enjoying being here, and I know I will enjoy talking with you!" Then I say with joy, "Give me a stage, a spotlight, a good microphone, and an enthusiastic audience, and I'm a happy boy!" And I say it with conviction, not anticipation! I mean it! I know it sounds rather self-serving, but it works, and helps to warm up the audience—and me.

The problem with public speaking, however, is that it causes people to experience a sense of vulnerability. We are, for better or worse, exposing ourselves to an audience who can independently pass judgment on us and our ability to present ourselves before them, on what we say, and on how we say it. But we can, with experience, develop tougher skin and get over that feeling. Remember, one way or another, we do survive!

We all become nervous before going on stage to speak. As I said earlier in this book, being nervous helps us to remain on top of our game. If we aren't nervous, we probably won't do our best job. Remember, you are only as good as your performance, and public speaking is, indeed, a performing art. We won't perform well unless we are nervous at least to some degree. As Mark Twain once said, "There are two types of public speakers, those who are nervous, and those who are liars." I have heard actors admit that if they ever find themselves not being nervous before a performance, it is time for them to quit.

So, hopefully through reading the remainder of the pages of this chapter, you will gain insights on how to overcome your fear of public speaking. Once we get over the feelings of fear and have an inspiring message to share, we are on our way to becoming an effective and inspiring public speaker!

When a microphone is placed in front of me, I panic!

I find it amusing when I observe a speaker who is handed a microphone so that she or he can be heard by those in the audience at the meeting or conference, and the hand that was given the microphone is often suddenly dropped to below the waist or held at arm's length in front of their chest. It appears that the speaker is attempting to keep the microphone as far away as possible from their mouth. When asked to hold the microphone closer so that he or she can be heard, the speaker may be seen to slowly and gingerly bring it closer to their mouth as though it may bite if it comes too close!

Or, when a lapel microphone is pinned to the shirt, tie, or blouse of the speaker, it seems all too frequently to be placed at or around the area of the speaker's belt or near the bottom of their tie, not realizing that at that distance from the speaker's mouth, it will not respond to their voice! Or, when a speaker who is asked to speak from a podium on which a flexible "gooseneck" is attached that holds a well-designed microphone, some speakers tend to move as far away as possible from it so as not to be heard by the audience. How sad it is that a speaker who came to present an important message appears to not want to be heard!

It is interesting to observe speakers who walk to the podium and say directly into the microphone that they are happy to be there, and then promptly walk away from the podium and the microphone as though they did not realize that it was placed there so that the audience could hear what they had to say! It is further disturbing to hear them say, "I won't need to use the microphone because people can always hear what I am saying." I tell my audiences to raise their hand and say loudly, "Please use the microphone so we can hear you!"

I often wonder why there is so much fear that surrounds a small piece of electronic equipment called a microphone. It certainly won't hurt you! It isn't dangerous in any way unless a heavy microphone is dropped on your foot! I think it has to do with an innate fear that many people seem to have that is caused by the fact that those in the audience can actually *hear* what they have to say!

That, to me, is difficult to comprehend; if we are speaking in front of an audience, we should *want* to be heard! Why else would we be there? It is frustrating when I observe speakers who have an audience in front of them who are there for the purpose of hearing what they have to say, apparently attempting to "hide" from the audience by refusing to be heard because they seem to be afraid of using the microphone! It doesn't matter if we are speaking before an audience of 500 or reading the minutes of the previous meeting or the financial report at a gathering of a local organization, the proper use of a microphone is essential to effective public speaking! I suppose, however, that they perhaps don't know *how* to use it properly.

The next section of this chapter offers suggestions on how to make yourself heard when using a microphone. That is, using it in such a way that it assures that you will be heard by those in your audience.

Now, if I'm not supposed to be afraid of microphones, how do I use them so that I don't embarrass myself?

There is nothing magical about microphones. They are designed to respond to sound waves that come from our mouth or other sources, give those sound waves a little boost, and then send that signal on to the amplifier of the PA system that the microphone is attached to.

However, there are different types of microphones. There are *dynamic microphones*; *condenser microphones*; *wireless microphones* that transmit our speech signal by way of an FM signal to the amplifier; *hard-wire microphones* that are hard-wired directly into the amplifier; *lapel microphones* that are designed so that the speaker does not have to hold a microphone, but are pinned to the shirt or blouse of the speaker; and *microphones that are permanently attached* to a podium by way of what is called a "goose-neck" holder. Those are convenient if the speaker is tied to notes and/or likes the security of standing behind a podium. Microphones, if used properly, do their job of transmitting our voice to the amplifier so that those in the audience can hear us.

Most microphones that are found in auditoriums, churches, and meeting rooms are *high-impedance microphones*. What does that mean? Well, if you know what the term *impede* means, then you are on your way to knowing what the microphone is designed to do. To impede, of course, means to restrict or resist. The word *high* would refer to highly restrictive or to greatly impede. In other words, the microphone is designed to restrict or impede the acoustic signal that is emitted from the mouth or perhaps a musical instrument.

The primary reason for that design is simple functionality. For example, if a singer is on stage with a "backup band" behind her or him, and there are amplifiers and electronic instruments used by the band, if the microphone did not restrict those electrical signals from the band that are also on stage with the singer, they tend to feed back into the singer's microphone and cause whistling and ringing sounds. You know what those are—the bothersome whistling or ringing sounds you have heard from time to time coming from the PA system speakers. So sound engineers have designed microphones to restrict those stray electrical and acoustic signals from being picked up by the singer's microphone.

Here's the clincher!

Most churches, auditoriums, and meeting rooms are equipped with those high-impedance microphones, so speakers must be aware of how to speak into them. Because those microphones restrict or impede the sounds of speech, the speaker's mouth must not be more than three to four inches from the microphone! That's where the "fear factor" comes into play. Don't be afraid! The microphone is guaranteed not to bite!

If you happen to have a lapel microphone that the person in charge of the meeting has pinned to your necktie or to your blouse, make sure that it is pinned, for men, to your collar, *not* the bottom of the shirt or necktie. If you are a woman and you happen to have worn your new low-neck dress, ask for a scarf of some type and pin the microphone up near your chin. Or, better yet, ask ahead of time about the type of microphone you will be using. You will avoid embarrassments that way.

If the microphone happens to be attached to a podium by way of a gooseneck holder, you have a choice. You can move the microphone by way of the gooseneck to within three inches from your mouth, or you can simply remove the microphone from the clamp that is holding the microphone to the gooseneck holder and hold the microphone in your hand.

I stipulated three to four inches from the mouth as the best distance for a standard high-impedance microphone. That is the usual distance. Experiment before you begin your presentation, preferably before the audience arrives. Amplification systems vary, of course, so three to four inches may be a little close. Five inches may be better for that specific system. In other words, experiment before you begin your presentation. I try to arrive at my speaking engagements at least thirty minutes early. Even if there are some people already sitting in the audience, experiment anyway and see how far or how close the microphone needs to be for the best quality of sound. You can use those who arrived early for your "sound checkers" by talking with them as the sound system is being adjusted to an appropriate level.

Some people say that I talk too fast. How fast should I speak so people can hear and understand me comfortably?

I, personally, actually become fatigued while listening to certain speakers. They speak with such great speed that my listening system (my brain) becomes tired! I actually despise listening to certain people who appear to take delight in speaking "trippingly on the tongue." I am asked from time to time to work with television news broadcasters and television weathermen about whom the news director of that television station has received complaints from viewers about the problems they experience understanding what they are saying. Whenever I begin working with them, I always ask them to bring with them a DVD or tape of one of their recent broadcasts so I can listen to it. I listen to their manner of enunciation, their vocal pitch, and I count the number of words per minute spoken by them. I am not really surprised anymore to find that many of them are speaking at a rate of around 200 words per minute!

The auditory portion of the human central nervous system (the brain) is simply not designed to understand speech that is spoken at that rapid of a pace. Human spoken speech is an extremely complex combination of sounds and pauses and inflectional clues—some sounds of speech are silent, others sound like hisses, others sound like small explosions, and others sound like partial guttural utterances. When speech is spoken at 200 words per minute (WPM), sentences are no longer sentences. Sentences become one long word. For example, if I said "The boy was running down the street" at 200 WPM, it would resemble, "Deboiwasrungdwndastret," and if combined with other sentences as the speaker continued, we would certainly not be able to keep up with what was being said!

The auditory portion of the human central nervous system is designed to comprehend adult spoken speech at a rate of around 126 words per minute (WPM). That is, for optimal speech understanding. At that speed, we begin to speak in whole words. All of the sounds necessary to pronounce the words become readily audible. Speech becomes much clearer! It is a wonderful experience, because the listener can actually understand what the speaker is saying!

Mr. Roger's Neighborhood

Have you ever had the pleasure of watching *Mr. Roger's Neighborhood* on television? Sadly, Fred Rogers passed away a number of years ago, but happily, his program can still be seen on public television. Fred Rogers was probably one of the only adults whom children could understand without difficulty. Three-year-old children were mesmerized by him, and they could actually tell their parents what happened during the program. That was primarily because they could understand what he was saying! The reason? The reason is because he was speaking at a rate that allowed their developing central nervous system to comprehend what he was saying!

Sadly, elementary school teachers, parents, and others children listen to generally speak at speeds upward of 160 to 180 WPM. It becomes impossible for children to understand adult spoken speech when it is spoken at those rates. It also becomes extremely difficult for adults!

Now, what does that have to do with adults speaking on stage to an audience of adults? I'll begin by asking if you remember Walter Cronkite and Tom Brokaw, the news commentators? Viewers loved to watch their television news broadcasts because viewers could understand what they were saying with ease. The reason? They, too, rehearsed speaking at a rate of approximately 126 words per minute during their news broadcasts—very close to that of Fred Rogers. I doubt if they had studied the human central nervous system and the optimal speed of speech that it can comprehend with greatest ease. But somehow, they surmised that a slower rate of speech allows listeners to hear and understand what they were saying with greater ease. Most successful television news broadcasters speak at rates that are slow enough to permit adults to understand, or perhaps I should say comprehend them. Beside their personality, their wit, and their body language (their presence) in front of a camera and microphone, it was their manner of presentation that drew audiences and television producers to them.

No wonder viewers call in to radio and television stations to complain that they have difficulty understanding what local news broadcasters are saying! Somehow, someone may have told the news commentators that speaking "trippingly on the tongue" would make them sound more intelligent or more knowledgeable! That is certainly not true, particularly when one cannot understand what they are saying! Or, perhaps they learned public speaking from each other, and those they learned from were poor models of clear and articulate speech.

Again, I have studied the speed of speech of adults across the U.S., including teachers, parents, salespersons, politicians, typical everyday adults, and others, and the average speed of speech I have measured is in the range of 160 to 180 WPM. Even at those speeds of utterance, it is very difficult for the average adult to hear and interpret what people are saying. The human central nervous system (the brain and its components that allow for interpretation or comprehension of spoken speech) is designed to be able to comprehend adult spoken speech when it is spoken at the rates that Fred Rogers, Walter Cronkite, and Tom Brokaw used—124 to 126 WPM. It seems quite slow to most speakers, but if we want listeners to understand what we are saying, that is the speed of speech that we must become accustomed to use.

What about using visual aids such as Power Point? Are there rules for that too?

According to Andrew Bradbury in his book entitled, *Successful Presentation Skills*, there are rules that, if followed, will make your visual aids more powerful and effective.[1] Today, Power Point is probably the most widely used form of visual aid. As with any visual aid, it can be used well, and it can be abused. For example, the phrase, "death by Power Point" describes instances in which Power Point is most dramatically abused. That phrase was used to describe a presentation at the Pentagon during which war strategies were being described and discussed. The slide in question contained so many intersecting dotted lines, arrows, cross-hatched

lines, and multiple miniature diagrams that were extremely difficult to read, that one military officer said to the one sitting next
to him, "If we ever figure out what that Power Point slide means,
we should be able to confuse the enemy enough to win the war!"
His points are as follows:

1. If possible, produce one slide that includes *all* points
    that you are going to cover in your presentation.
    Confine the material on the slide to only four or
    five points, with no more than five words per point.
    However, that is sometimes not possible.

2. Review the slide to make sure that it can be read in
    its entirety in approximately six seconds.

3. If it takes much more than six seconds to read a par-
    ticular slide, then it needs editing!

4. Check to see how much of the text (if any) is simply
    a direct copy of what you will be saying in that part
    of your presentation. The slide should not be a di-
    rect copy of the words you will be saying, but rather
    simply the points you intend to cover in your narra-
    tive presentation.

5. Cross out everything that isn't absolutely necessary.
    If you still have anything longer than key words or
    phrases, then you haven't finished editing.

6. If more than four or five bullet points are left, either
    merge some of the points or split them up over sev-
    eral slides.

7. If a rehearsal of your presentation leaves you changing slides almost as fast as you can speak, perhaps the information on each slide is too brief. It is okay to take material from two slides and combine it onto a single slide.

Other pointers on the use of Power Point and other visual aids

1. Don't turn your back to your audience in order to see the screen that contains your visuals. Position yourself so that you can see the audience, but at the same time see the projection screen. Or, position the computer that holds your slides so that you can see the computer screen from time to time.

2. Don't ever read from the screen! The audience knows how to read! It is up to you to interpret what is written on your visuals. Some of the most boring presentations are those during which the speaker stands on the stage and reads the slides to the audience. You are there to make a presentation, not to prove that you know how to read!

3. Unless there is detail on your slides that represents logistical areas of a battlefield or a description of a new shopping center, pointers or laser pointers are not necessary. They can be a distraction, not a help.

Note

1. Andrew Bradbury, *Successful Presentation Skills* (London: Kogan Page, 2006).

CHAPTER 10

PRODUCTIVE COMMUNICATIONS

We've all heard it said that no one is an island. This phrase has become such an integral part of our vernacular that we often forget how profound it is. Any success, significance, or satisfaction we achieve in our personal or professional lives depends on quality involvement by other people. This quality involvement is only possible if we have ongoing, successful, two-way communications.

Several years ago during a conversation with Steve Forbes, we began discussing the concept of productivity. Productivity is something we all seek. It is the effective ongoing pursuit of a worthwhile and significant goal. Our conversation grew and built to the point where we determined to write a book. Mr. Forbes and I agreed that productivity is not possible without great teamwork, so I reached out to arguably the best team builder of the 20th century, my friend and colleague Coach John Wooden.

Coach Wooden had become a legend for literally rewriting the college basketball record books while amassing an unprecedented number of national championships. Even though Coach Wooden was 98 years old when we began the discussions that would culminate in my book *Ultimate Productivity*, his great mind functioned at a level we should all aspire to achieve.

I've heard it said of learned people that they "have forgotten more than most people know." This would have been true of Coach Wooden except it seemed that he had not forgotten anything. We lost John Wooden just short of his 100th birthday, but his records, lessons, and teachings live on and inspire us all.

Mr. Forbes wrote the foreword to *Ultimate Productivity* and, along with Coach Wooden, provided much of the wisdom and experience that made the book possible. We agreed that productivity must be broken down into its three components—motivation, communication, and implementation.

Without motivation, nothing that we would call success or productivity is even possible. People are motivated by recognition, money, inclusion, significance, legacy, and many other factors. As Coach Wooden said, "Some of my players were motivated by a gentle pat on the back; others needed to be patted a little lower and a lot harder."

If productivity begins with motivation, it certainly culminates with implementation. We live in a world where, when it's all said and done, there's a great deal said and very little done. Productive people implement in a variety of methods. Some people multitask while others work in a linear fashion from one step to the next. Some people work as part of an ongoing team while others need to work in isolation and then bring their contribution to the team.

It is important that we find out what motivates everyone around us and how they best implement as we move toward our mutual goals. The bridge between motivation and implementation is communication. If, indeed, no one is an island, the bridge from our island to the rest of the world is our ability to communicate with others and have them communicate with us.

Just as we determined that people are motivated by different factors and implement in different ways, in researching *Ultimate Productivity*, we came to understand that everyone in your personal and professional lives will communicate in different ways. Coach Wooden drew on his decades of experience with basketball players to explain that some players need to see a play drawn up on the board while you can just tell other players what to do, and still other players need to walk through the play on the basketball floor.

The people you communicate with on a daily basis communicate best in a variety of ways. Some people need it in writing, others need to repeat it back to you, and still others need to walk through the concept you are discussing. A "one-size-fits-all" approach to communication will leave many people frustrated, and much of the detail you are trying to communicate will be lost.

If you or anyone with whom you live or work would like to determine and be able to share the methods of motivation, communication, and implementation that are the most productive for each individual, you can take my productivity assessment and get a free productivity profile by simply going to www .UltimateProductivity.com and using the access code 586404. The profile may seem simplistic to you or some of the people around you if you are an effective communicator; however, we have shared the productivity profile with top executives in *Fortune* 500 companies, military and political leaders, entrepreneurs, and many others, and they have all found hidden elements that can help them improve and will help you, your loved ones, and your colleagues.

My co-author, Dr. Ray Hull, is a recognized expert in the field of communications. One of the elements of his expertise that originally attracted me to his work was his study of speaking at the appropriate speed. I sat in a U.S. Department of Education workshop conducted by Dr. Hull in Washington, DC, in which he explained to lifelong educators and those who train educators that we must speak to children, adolescents, and adults at different speeds. Most of us intuitively understand that we must use a different vocabulary when speaking to a six-year-old as opposed to a sixty-year-old; but none of us who attended Dr. Hull's workshop had thought much, if any, about the rate at which we speak.

Most teachers and parents have had the experience of telling a child to do something only to have their instructions ignored. This often results in frustration and a louder, more rapid-fire repeat of the instructions to the child. This is invariably met with a blank stare, and what the parent or teacher might take for defiance or stubbornness on the part of the child is simply the child's inability to understand the instructions spoken at an accelerated pace.

The first time I experienced Ray Hull demonstrating a variety of speech rates of speed, I was profoundly impacted because for a quarter of a century as the founder and president of the Narrative Television Network, I had been involved in making movies, television, and educational programming for children accessible for blind and visually impaired audiences.

The process of describing or narrating video programming involves inserting lines of description between the existing dialogue in the programming. Oftentimes, there are only a few seconds in which to describe many details, so our narrators had traditionally spoken very quickly. After beginning the collaboration with Ray Hull that has resulted in this book, we at the Narrative Television Network have developed a three-tiered description system in which we narrate programs for elementary students, middle-school students, and high-school students at different rates of speed using appropriate vocabulary. While this may seem self-evident as you read these words, I am humbled to admit that, as a blind person myself, providing this accessibility service to young people and adults for a quarter of a century, we had never dealt with the elements of communication that Dr. Ray Hull introduced to us.

During the writing of this book, I took a trip to Las Vegas for a speaking engagement. As the plane descended and approached the Las Vegas airport, Hoover Dam was visible from the left side of the airplane. The copilot emerged from the cockpit and spoke to a few passengers at the front of the plane as they were looking at Hoover Dam and Lake Mead far below. This pilot explained to several people that he has flown this route at least twice a week for many years, and he began to share facts about Hoover Dam with several passengers.

To a gentleman who seemed like a middle-aged businessman, he explained how much the government had spent to build the dam, but the project had been completed two years early and under budget. When a retired lady commented on how big the dam was, the copilot mentioned that several of the workmen had died while working on the project, and there were memorial plaques on the dam itself, placed there as a tribute to these fallen workers. To an eight-year-old boy who had just exclaimed rather loudly, "Hey, Mom. Look at that!" the copilot said, "Son, do you realize there's enough concrete in that dam to build a two-lane highway from the Atlantic Ocean all the way across the country to the Pacific Ocean?"

As I sat across the aisle on that flight listening to the copilot conversing with his various passengers, I realized he was sharing facts that were pertinent to each individual, and he was sharing them in an age-appropriate manner. When we communicate with others, we are often so busy worrying about what we want to say that we fail to think about how it should be said and in what way the communication can best be delivered to that individual. Today, I am proud to say that as the Narrative Television Network enters its second quarter century, we are in tune with the specific needs of the audience for which the program is intended.

When we are communicating with people in an attempt to be productive, it is critical that we assess whether our goals and the other person's are the same. There are some people who have a different agenda, and it is best on certain occasions to be cautious with our communications or, on rare occasions, to not even communicate at all.

Several years ago, I was asked to speak at the National Day of Prayer in Washington, DC, and while I was in town, the Wounded Warriors organization asked if I would be willing to come to Ft. Belvoir and make a speech for them. There are some people to whom we owe a debt we can never pay, and to this end, I always try to take every opportunity to assist groups like the Wounded Warriors.

When my colleague and I reached the base, we were greeted by a colonel who gave us a tour of Ft. Belvoir, then introduced us to the commanding officer of the base who was seated at the head table for the event where I would be speaking. The general and I had a pleasant and fascinating conversation and then he introduced me for my speech.

After the event, the general walked my colleague and me to the car that would be taking us to the airport. As we approached the vehicle, we were confronted by a reporter who fired several hostile questions at us. He asked if I had ever served in the military; was I ordained and, therefore, qualified to speak at the National Day of Prayer; and several other questions that I felt were intended more to trip me up and create a sound bite than to elicit effective and accurate communication. The general informed the reporter in a very direct and impactful way that generals have of communicating that there would be no questions and no comments.

As the general and I were saying goodbye at the car, he told me that same reporter had confronted him several times with hostile comments. He said the reporter had accused him of institutionalizing violence. The general and I both agreed that comment would be the basis of a fascinating discussion if the reporter were really seeking insight and not just inflammatory headlines. Before you answer anyone's questions, it is imperative that you understand why they want to know and what they are going to do with the information.

When we are in court, we are compelled to tell the truth, the whole truth, and nothing but the truth. There are other times when we certainly tell the truth, but the person or situation does not require us to tell the whole truth; and then there are hostile situations in which the best form of communication may be to clearly communicate, "No comment." All of us want to be productive and communicate effectively, but there are times when we must cut off communications in order to be productive and, therefore, communicate on a higher level or a more targeted manner.

I have written 30 books to date, and at this writing there are more than 10 million copies of my books in print in two dozen languages. In each of those books, including this one, I provide my phone number for readers who may need more information, inspiration, or details. If you find that you are one of those individuals, you can reach me at 918-627-1000 or email Jim@JimStovall.com. Because my contact information is so readily available, our office receives many sales calls, solicitations, political calls, and individuals phoning for all manner of self-serving reasons that have nothing to do with the mission and goals that my team and I have.

In many organizations, the most entry-level, junior person can be found at the front desk. That is not the case at the Narrative Television Network where our phones are answered and our guests coming in the front door are greeted by an eminently talented professional named Beth Sharp. Beth writes scripts for movie and television shows we are narrating, and she organizes our office and all the projects we undertake as well as serving as a receptionist. She has an uncanny and unfailing ability to screen phone calls and determine within a few seconds whether it's one of my readers or a sales call from someone wanting to take my time and distract me from the things I should be doing to pay attention to their agenda. Beth politely and professionally puts the calls from my readers through to me and efficiently gets rid of the other callers.

Great communication does not only involve effectively exchanging thoughts and ideas with other people, but it demands that we keep our goals and ideals in mind when we determine who we are going to communicate with. We all only have 24 hours in each day, and there are times when we can't communicate with everyone who wants to communicate with us. This makes it imperative that we perform a sort of communication triage in which we determine which channel of communication will allow us to do the most good for the most people while being the most productive in reaching our goals.

Part of communication triage involves assessing the manner of our verbal and nonverbal communications. We've all had the experience of being around a young child who falls down or bumps into something. They invariably look to us to determine whether or not they are really hurt. If we panic and rush over to them as if they are mortally wounded, they will cry and wail as if it were their last breath on earth. On the other hand, if we calmly approach them and help them up as if it's the most normal thing that occurs every day, they will assume they are not injured and calmly go about their business.

This type of calming verbal and nonverbal communication is critical for leaders, pilots, surgeons, and anyone who performs vital tasks in high-pressure situations. We all watch the presidential debates so we can feel informed and determine how to cast our votes. In the final analysis, when voters' feedback is evaluated by experts, it is revealed that it is not as important what a candidate said or even how well they said it as long as they seem to communicate with this intangible quality we call "presidential." Being "presidential" communicates verbally and nonverbally that one is in control, knows what to do, and has the ability to get it done.

In effective communications, we must calibrate what we say as well as what is said to us. There are times I find it helpful to assign numbers to certain people's statements. For a number of years, I have been a part of an informal investment group made up of 30 or 40 investors. Periodically, we come together and buy a piece of real estate, a commercial development, or an emerging business. There are some members of our group who are perpetually exuberant and enthusiastic. When presented with an opportunity, they might jump out of their chair, pound the table, and exclaim, "This deal can't lose! We should put everything we have into it and mortgage our homes to get more money to invest in this deal."

This type of communication can be misleading if you don't calibrate what you're hearing based on who you are hearing from. There are people in our group who make such exuberant statements several times a week even when referring to fairly average, mundane investments. On a scale of one to ten, with ten being total commitment to make the investment, and one being *we should not invest under any circumstance*, the enthusiastic individual mentioned above might only be calibrated numerically at a five or six. On the other hand, there are very conservative members of our investment group who, when presented with the same opportunity, might mutter, "Well, if we invested in that, we probably wouldn't lose all our money." After calibrating this individual's communication based on past experience, I might give them an eight or even a nine on the investment scale. We cannot just look at what is said or even how it's said because different words mean different things from different individuals.

If we are to be productive in our communications and in our lives, we must keep in mind not only where we want to go, but also, we must be mindful of the goals and objectives of others. My late, great friend and mentor Zig Ziglar was fond of saying, "You can get everything out of life you want if you'll just help enough other people get what they want."

The highest form of productive communication not only allows us to share our thoughts, feelings, goals, and aspirations with others, but it gives us the privilege of learning what matters to them and how we can become a part of it.

CHAPTER 11

THE ART OF PUBLIC RELATIONS AND IMAGE

People make their living by assisting others to develop their personal and professional image. Interestingly, the field of public relations is nearly an industry unto itself. Good image builders and public relations experts stand to make a sizeable income assisting others to enhance their businesses, enhance their ability to impress their current and potential customers, enhance their advertising acumen, or enhance the stature of their business.

Our ability to impress our customers—our clients—-makes or breaks our business or our practice whether it be a commercial enterprise, a dental practice, or a church where the minister is the center of focus. Here, I am referring to our ability to demonstrate the high quality of what we do every day, and the sincerity of effort that drives what we do in the long term. If the services that we are providing are of the highest quality and we demonstrate the knowledge and skill that is necessary to assure the public that we are capable of maintaining a high quality of our services, then we should do well.

I will emphasize the word *should* in the sentence above. The reason? The reason is that there are many in businesses and medical and non-medical practices including hairdressers, plumbers, electricians, salespeople, masseuses, counselors, and on and on who possess the knowledge and skill to be a success, but do not achieve the level that they should be able to achieve because of the image that they portray and/or their ability to engage in the level of public relations that would allow them to achieve a high level of success.

How do we achieve the level of success we dream of? This chapter provides detail on the art of public relations and image— what is required to impress and to enhance not only our self-image, but also enhance the image of our practices or our businesses so that the world will recognize that we are what we are striving to become!

The processes entailed in enhancing our professional image and the art of public relations involves communication at one of its highest levels! Within that process, we are communicating to the world in order to promote our businesses or our practices, so that we can hopefully achieve our highest level of success.

I am told that the image that we portray says who we really are. What can I do to enhance my image?

We are what we are. Does that make sense? In other words, we are how we present ourselves. As I said in an earlier chapter, body language comprises at least 70 percent of what we say. That is, how we appear, how we act, how we dress, how we sit, the gestures we use, the jewelry we wear, the way we walk into a room, the hygiene we practice, and so many others that they are difficult to list. They are all important parts of "communication." We are communicating to others who and what we are and what we represent!

For example, let's look at the matter of personal appearance—that is, how we dress, how we appear. How we first appear as we enter a room can make or break the impression we desire to make. The "two minute rule" referred to in Chapter 5 applies here. The impression we make when we enter a room and walk to our potential customer, our patient, or our client is generally solidified in about two minutes. That first impression is difficult to erase.

So, how should we dress? Here are some pointers.

For Women

- **Conservative clothing is a must**. No miniskirts, no blouses that reveal more than a slight area below the neck. A suit, either pantsuit or other business attire, is very appropriate. Anything less can be a detriment to you.

- **Simple accessories**. No heavy jewelry, no matter what you are used to wearing; no multiple bracelets or rings. Jewelry should be so discreetly worn that it will only be noticed as appropriate and does not draw attention to itself. You want attention to be drawn to **you**—not your jewelry.

- **Comfortable shoes**. No four-inch spike heels or three-inch platform shoes that only make others in the room wonder just how you are able to walk without falling!

- **Discreet makeup**. Avoid heavy eye shadow, false eyelashes, heavy luminescent lipstick, or heavy use of rouge.

- **Appropriate hair grooming**. At all costs avoid spiked and obviously dyed hair including pink or green or blue, bright red hair, or other vivid colors. Avoid the avant-garde look that can happen when your hairstylist tries some new experimental ideas or techniques with your hair. Conservative hair styles give one an air of sophistication and good taste.

- **No face piercings, nose or lip rings, or multiple ear piercings, ear spikes or ear gauges.** And, if your naval is pierced, or even if it is not, cover it up!

- **No visible tattoos**. Tattoos do not impress those who may be served by you in your business or your practice. In fact, there are many adults who will avoid associating with you or allowing you to serve them through your business or practice if they see tattoos that are obviously being hidden by the clothing you are wearing. The best way to avoid having to try to hide tattoos is to avoid having them done in the first place!

For Men

Here are some pointers for men regarding appearance in business or in your practice. Some are the same as pointed out for women, but others are designed specifically for men. For example:

- **Conservative clothing is a must**. A sport jacket and slacks with a shirt of a conservative color—white, blue, tan—is always appropriate. On days when casual clothing is the mode of dress and those whom you will be serving are made aware of it, then a casual sport jacket, white shirt, well-designed blue jeans, white socks, and penny loafers can be very appropriate.

- **Avoid pins and ties that convey political or religious affiliations.** Although they may have significant meaning in your life, they may not for others. In fact, they can be the igniter of arguments if another person you may be talking with sees them as offensive or as a challenge to their beliefs.

- **Wear non-distracting jewelry.** A man who wears multiple rings on their fingers, necklaces, and other such jewelry is, for some people, considered to be "showing off" or not to be trusted.

- **Wear conservative and well-groomed shoes**. White or baby blue patent leather shoes definitely do not impress, no matter how nice they looked in the store window! Well-groomed and polished shoes, either tie or loafers, are always appropriate. Dark brown or black are most easily matched to the clothes worn by well-groomed men; wear with matching socks.

- **Clean hands and clean fingernails are always important**. Make sure that your fingernails are clean and trimmed to within an eighth of an inch from the tips of your fingers. Nails that are too long give hands a feminine appearance (unless you are a flamenco guitar player). Nails that have dirt under them are definitely not impressive, nor are hands that need washing.

- **No face piercing including nose and lip rings or tongue spikes**. Even though they may be in style, they can be repulsive to many people, and those may have been your potential customers or clients or patients!

- **No multiple pierced ear rings, ear lobe gauges, or spikes**. Again, even though they may be in style, they can be a significant "turn off" to many people. Any ear rings on men, no matter how small, can be a negative distraction to your potential customers, clients, or patients.

- **Visible tattoos are a no-no**. Again, as with women, visible tattoos can give negative impressions to potential customers. No matter how "in style" they are at the time, many people view them as being suspect. If you feel that you must have a tattoo, hopefully it can be covered when working with those you serve. I have observed both men and women with arms and legs and neck covered with tattoos, and all one can wonder is, "Why?"

Enhancing our professional image through our conduct with our clients and business associates: How do we do that?

The manner in which we conduct ourselves as we work with our clients and business associates can profoundly influence our effectiveness in the day-to-day routine of our professional lives. It involves our ability to communicate with those with whom we associate and work. It involves who we are and how we respond to the needs of our customers and our business associates. It is a critically important part of this activity we call "interpersonal communication." So, what are some suggestions that would enhance our image and our ability to do well in the area of public relations?

Here are some of those suggestions regarding conduct with clients and business associates:

Conduct with Clients and Business Associates

- *Be punctual for meetings and appointments.* However, *don't* be too early if you have an appointment with your boss. By "too early" I mean fifteen minutes early. It does nothing for public relations with your boss or other important person if we stick our head into their office fifteen minutes before your meeting time, with "I know I'm early, but I was hoping we could begin," and your boss is trying desperately to finish composing a letter that she wanted to send via email before your meeting started! If you arrive early, be polite by informing the receptionist that you have arrived for your meeting, but that you are early, and then simply sit patiently in a nearby waiting area until the appointed time of your meeting.

- Be polite, no matter how bad the day. Don't take your bad day out on your clients by telling them about it!

- Be appropriate in all behaviors—no off-color jokes or remarks no matter how innocent they appear to you.

- Be pleasant, be a genuinely good person, be empathetic, be nice!

- Be a good ambassador to your field.

- If a client comes to you wanting their money returned or is making some other demand that you may think is not reasonable, no matter what the reason, think—if I were the client or associate, how would I want this handled?

- How would I respond if that person was my relative or my friend? Then, handle it that way.

- Always remember this rule: We are here to serve, not to judge.

- Work hard to be a flexible and creative problem solver.

- Affirm your commitment to helping people and how much you enjoy the opportunity!

Enhancing our professional image through our communication skills with clients and business associates: What are some suggestions?

Chapter 9 was, of course, on the topic of "The Art of Speaking Before an Audience," which involves skill in communication, and Chapter 5 was on the topic of "The Art of Nonverbal Communication," while Chapter 7 was on the topic of "The Art of Constructive Listening." All of those are important in relation to our ability to communicate with our clients and associates on a day-to-day basis. All of those important elements of communication work together to assist us in being good communicators in our daily life at work and at home.

Here are some suggestions that if followed, will not only assist you in building a good professional image, but also assist you in building excellent public relations for your business or practice:

Communication Skills with Clients and Business Associates

- Listen carefully and quietly to what the other person is saying, no matter how urgently you want them to know that you have the solution to their problem!

It's important for the other person to fully express her or himself before you interject your suggestions.

- Be carefully attentive to what the other person is saying to you—no side glances or wandering eyes.

- Again, when listening, do not interrupt, but reflect your feelings through facial expressions and an occasional nod while maintaining good eye contact with the one who is speaking to you.

- Be empathetic, but not in a demeaning manner. Never respond by saying, "I know just how you feel," unless you have clearly experienced what the other person is expressing.

- Remember to speak at a slightly slower rate than your usual speed of speech. You will be much more easily understood.

- When you slow your rate of speech, a natural response that is generally noticed is that you will articulate with greater clarity. Just do not over-articulate. That can be embarrassing to the one with whom you are speaking.

- Maintain good eye contact, but do not stare at the person you are speaking with. For best eye contact, concentrate on the other person's nose. As I said in Chapter 5, do *not* look into their eyes. That level of intimacy is not appropriate unless you intend to ask her or him to marry you!

The appearance of our work environment and staff conduct enhances our professional image and is an important component of business communication.

The appearance that we design for our work environment and the conduct of our staff members further enhances the positive public relations we desire to create. It is the final ingredient that accompanies our desire for a positive personal/professional image and the design that we have created in order to achieve that image.

Here are some suggestions that will assist in creating a positive office design and suggestions to assist staff in their conduct with your clients:

- Clients and customers are positively influenced by tasteful office design and décor. Attractive furniture, drapes, and wall hangings are important. They influence how our clients and customers feel about us and the services that we offer on their behalf.

- Use color that is calming and relaxing. Mauve, rose, lavender, and other calming colors are important. Bright and luminescent colors, while someone may have told you that those types of colors will keep customers happy and upbeat, can be exhausting to some older adults.

- Office furniture should not be too hard or too soft, and the furniture arrangement should not provide an obstacle course for your clients. I find it amusing sometimes when I go to an office where there is a waiting area filled with forty chairs and numerous coffee tables, and I am the only one in the room. It brings me to wonder if at one time the business or practice had that many customers, and for some reason they are not coming there anymore. It results in my feeling a little uneasy about being there. If the waiting area usually only requires six chairs and one coffee table with magazines on the top of the table, then keep your waiting area small enough so that if there are two people waiting, they won't feel as though the property was abandoned just before they arrived!

- Environmental design is critical for good communication with clients and customers, with adequate lighting that is not too bright or reflectant. It is important to use incandescent lighting rather than fluorescent. Fluorescent lighting is known to cause tearing of the eyes, restlessness, and even seizures in children and adults who have never before experienced a seizure. No matter how new the bulbs, they still emit an almost subliminal flicker. It is the flicker in fluorescent lights that causes the problems.

- Adequate and accessible parking is critical.

- Remember, the receptionist sets the tone and stage for everything in the business or practice. She or he should be financially compensated in accordance with their importance to the organization.

Staff must use all of the principles that I have discussed in this chapter regarding manner of dress, their personal appearance and demeanor, and their ability to communicate effectively with your customers or clients. If they do not, then it is our responsibility to teach them those important elements of image and skills in public relations. If they cannot seem to demonstrate them consistently, then we can either continue to remind them of those elements or suggest that perhaps they will do better at another place of employment.

CHAPTER 12

THE COMMUNICATION CATALOG

Complete, effective, and high-quality communication is much like a detailed recipe. All elements need to be in place and be handled properly if you are to enjoy a tasty meal or good communication.

We have all seen high-profile politicians, athletes, and celebrities who lose their fame and fortune due to one poorly executed or thoughtless communication. I remain mindful of Coach Wooden's powerful advice to his players. "You will be known for a lifetime of good things you do or one lapse of judgment."

Attention to detail is more important than ever here in the 21st century. The digital age has made it possible for us to communicate with virtually anyone, anywhere, at any time. This has greatly increased the potential for communication, but it has also increased noise, clutter, and interference.

It is so easy to send a digital communication, and it is impossible to take it back. Teenagers or young adults who think that fun, frivolous video footage from their Friday night party is something they need to share with all of their friends rarely think about the fact that future employers, partners, voters, and college admissions staff will have access to the scenes from their party for years to come.

Our brains are a marvelous gift. Psychological studies have shown that our memories fade and soften with respect to uncomfortable or unpleasant memories. Unfortunately, our digital memories will be as clear, stark, and in focus decades from now as they are today; therefore, communication and reputation management is of paramount importance.

Whenever you have a difficult conversation of either a personal or a professional nature, it is best to do it in person as any harsh or uncomfortable exchanges can have an opportunity to fade and settle into proper perspective over time. In the course of running several businesses, on rare occasions I have had the very unpleasant task of firing someone. I always do this myself in a face-to-face, private meeting, which is the same way I hired the person in the beginning.

Even when it is done compassionately, being fired is a difficult process, but I am grateful that the handful of people I have had to accompany through this process all remain friends of mine today. I suspect if I had fired them by voicemail, email, or a formal letter, we might not enjoy the cordial friendships we do today because those words would be in the same form and have the same force of emotion they had the day the firing occurred.

As a professional speaker, I am often asked to make appearances at Toastmasters clubs in my hometown. I try to honor as many of these requests as I can because I believe Toastmasters is an important organization which is dedicated to all aspects of public speaking and communication. At Toastmasters meetings over the years, I have met people from all walks of life who are working on various and specific aspects of their own speaking ability which they wish to improve. These meetings always remind me that communication is not one thing made up of one element but is a complex bouquet of individual parts that needs to all be pulled together to reach the highest possible impact.

One word, phrase, or gesture that is in poor taste or insensitive can ruin the communication and possibly a valuable personal or professional relationship. One, two, or three words can be powerful. I believe the most powerful word in our English language is the simple word *please*. The word *please* turns any command or order into a request.

I became a student of President Harry S. Truman when I wrote my first *Homecoming Historical* novel entitled *One Season of Hope*. Each of these novels is set in a high school which is named after a historical figure. In this series, my readers enjoy a modern-day inspirational drama that takes place in a high school with sporadic historical vignettes about the school's namesake spread throughout the novel.

While writing *One Season of Hope*, I got to work with The National Archives and the Truman Library to verify all of my facts and Truman quotes. One of the most timely and timeless statements made by Harry Truman was when he announced to the world after World War II that "Americans will give millions for charity but not one single penny for tribute." What Truman meant as he spoke to a war-ravaged world with many countries seeking aid from the U.S. was that America would give all it could to those who asked but would not give anything to those who felt they were entitled to take resources from our country.

A demand can turn into a request by just adding the simple word *please*.

If you only have two words to use and want to make the maximum impact on the job or in your home, it would be hard to find two more powerful words than *thank you*. *Thank you* can be communicated in many forms beyond just uttering the two words. The highest performing corporate executives, managers, and salespeople often employ handwritten thank-you notes. The fact that some people think that a handwritten note is outdated and antiquated makes it more impactful for those who use this powerful tool.

You should not only thank those who buy what you're selling or choose to do business with you. You should constantly thank those who work with you and even those from whom you buy products and services. Many business leaders are shocked when I tell them to thank their vendors, but I am a big believer in catching people doing something right. Whether it's the president of my bank, the head of an airline, or the maintenance man in my building, a simple thank-you note to them or their boss can make all the difference now and in the future.

I frequently enclose thank-you notes with checks as I am paying bills. Businesspeople who follow this practice will stand out among the crowd because it is so rare. Another form of *thank you* with my vendors is paying my bills the day they arrive. Some economists might argue that I lose the interest float for a few weeks on the money, but I believe this pales in comparison to the advantages I receive when I call on my vendors for rush orders, special favors, or extended service. The people I work with across the country and around the world know me and remember me because I'm the guy who sincerely shared the two powerful words with them—*thank you.*

If you only have three words to use and you want to make the highest possible impact, the magic words are *I love you.* Ironically, these words can actually express an emotion and create an emotion. These three little words are used far too often and should extend far beyond our spouse, soul mate, or significant other. *I love you* should be the beginning and end of any difficult conversation with a friend or family member. People need to be reminded that what we're talking about is a product of what we think. The phrase *I love you* is a product of what we feel.

For the same reason that many difficult or uncomfortable confrontational conversations should not be put in writing, the phrase *I love you* and the details that go along with those three words should be put in writing and memorialized in other ways. Our parents and grandparents, having no access to what we enjoy in the digital age and having limited access to telephones, wrote detailed and thoughtful letters. These letters not only communicated their emotions in the moment but served as reminders of that moment for the rest of their lives and for generations to come.

Many of us know about our parents or great-grandparents because of letters they wrote back and forth to one another during decades gone by. One has to wonder what our children or grandchildren will have of us in generations to come. Among my most valued possessions are letters that my father wrote to me when I was a teenager and a young adult. He didn't need to send me a letter for logistical reasons as my bedroom was a few feet down the hall from his, but I think he wanted to ponder his communication before presenting it to me, and I believe he understood that I would have those letters with me throughout my life, and they would serve people even beyond me.

This book and each of my other 30 titles have been dictated to a talented and valued colleague named Dorothy Thompson. My hundreds of weekly columns, screenplays for the movies based on my books, and all of my novels and nonfiction titles would not exist without Dorothy. She is the best editor and grammarian I have ever encountered and has the uncanny ability to perform these tasks as I am dictating to her. My book publishers as well as the editors of the newspapers, magazines, and online publications around the world that carry my weekly columns know that if it comes out of my office, it's been edited and proofed by Dorothy, and therefore, it is ready to print.

Several years ago, Dorothy and I were working on one of my books when she got the call that her mother, who was in her 80s, was very ill and was not expected to live too long. Dorothy rushed to her hometown about 100 miles away and got to spend some quality time with her mother before she passed away. During that time, her mother told her about a box she would find on a shelf in her mother's home.

When the timing was appropriate, Dorothy and her sister opened that box and discovered that it was filled with poetry her mother had written throughout her life. When Dorothy told me about her mother's poetry, I asked her to share some of it with me, and I found it to be amazing in its depth and simplicity. Dorothy's mother's name was Joye Kanelakos, and I wrote a book that included her poetry with my perspective and commentary entitled *Discovering Joye*. By reducing her communication to writing and sharing it with her family, Joye not only impacted her loved ones but countless other people all around the world.

You and I have the opportunity to create and pass along a communication legacy. A scrapbook or just an envelope filled with old letters, articles, academic and professional commendations, and other memorabilia may seem useless to you, but it will be priceless to future generations.

The most powerful communication you can utter to another person in a personal or professional setting is their name. Just greeting them in this way shows that you hold them in a place of esteem, respect, and significance. A supreme insult or demonstration of disrespect is to repeatedly not remember someone's name. Certainly, we all struggle with this, and people understand when you can't remember their name in the early part of a relationship, but make it a priority to remember them and remember their name.

Beyond their name, you can greatly impact others when you remember who they are and what they do. When you can introduce people properly or put them in the appropriate context, it makes a tremendous difference in the ongoing communication.

As a professional speaker, I treasure those times when the master of ceremonies or the head of a corporation brings me onto the stage with a quality introduction. My staff sends the standard introduction I prefer to the people who organize each event where I'm speaking, and we also take one with us to the venue, but unfortunately, too many people have not discovered the hidden value of a great introduction.

If you are in an academic field or a specific profession, it is powerful when you can communicate with a note accompanying an article or other publicity in which someone is mentioned. Great communication begins with remembering, recognizing, and responding to others. It can't be overstated that people don't care how much you know until they know how much you care. I would never suggest that you should be insincere or gratuitous in your communications, but if you have sincere feelings of admiration, respect, or love for others, they are useless when you don't share them and priceless when you do.

CHAPTER 13

THE ART OF CONFLICT RESOLUTION

One of the most difficult challenges that we face in the process of interpersonal communication involves conflict resolution. Conflict resolution, I feel, involves more creativity, more flexibility, and more resilience than any other aspect of human communication. However, it is a form of communication in which every person who ventures forth into the company of others must, at some time or another, participate. According to Reardon, conflict resolution is necessitated by the fact that at some time or another, people differ in their goals or their apparent needs, and the means by which they attempt to achieve them.[1] The inevitable result is that their goals may be at cross purposes with those of another person.

One person's needs or goals may be blocked by the goal seeking of another person. Conflict resolution is one means of achieving resolution and cooperation.

Encouraging changes in another person's behavior or their means of achieving their needs or goals may be for the betterment of that person or the betterment of relationships. The person seeking resolution of the conflict can have as one of her or his goals the improvement of relationships, the resolution of conflicting goals between two people, or the improvement of a situation that, if left unattended, could deteriorate into a worsening conflict. The intent is not the betterment of the person seeking resolution, but rather the successful resolution of the conflict per se.

Conflict resolution involves a delicate form of communication. It first of all involves at least two people who may have differing opinions on how to achieve a goal, or differing opinions on how to achieve their or their organization's needs. It does not involve coercion because coercion involves some form of threat either to the person or to their sense of self-esteem. For example, children are sometimes coerced into behaving as adults would like for them to behave. While there are times when reasoning with children is not as important as removing them from immediate danger, using coercion in child rearing does not teach children to reason and solve problems on their own. They learn best by instruction and by example.

Conflict resolution is not something that one person does *to* another person, but rather something that is done *with* another person. What is involved in this activity?

The following will give the reader ideas on how to constructively engage in the resolution of conflict through interpersonal communication and how to resolve potential conflicts through indirect and sometimes direct interaction with those involved. A few of the strategies I have learned from my 17-year-old daughter who is a very wise young lady, and from my wife who is also a very wise individual. Others I have learned from my many years in administrative positions, positions of leadership, and many laboratories in interpersonal communication that involve strategies for resolution of conflict. Some of the strategies seem so logical that you will wonder why they are even included; others you may not have thought about, or felt that perhaps they involved too much effort. None of these require a great deal of effort, but sometimes they *do* require us to use the greatest amount of poise, charm, and patience that we can muster!

I have been involved in conflicts at work and at home, and for some reason, I usually turned the conflict into a greater one than it was in the beginning! What can I do to do a better job?

Here are some suggestions that should help in many situations in which conflict is evident:

- We must try our best to keep a sense of humor. Do *not* let the conflict become more serious than it deserves to be.

- Shoot for a suitable resolution. Or rather, the goal should be to reach a positive solution. Compromise and a willingness to give a little is oftentimes the key.

- We should express our feelings. If you feel resentful, say it. Keeping it bottled up may result in an explosion of emotion that will be regretted later.

- Communicate clearly and openly. Do not expect others to read your mind. This is true in business and in relationships including marriage. Think of a marriage partner who returns home empty-handed, when the spouse thought that he or she would remember to bring a loaf of bread home from the grocery store and says, "You should have known!" It is then common to hear the refrain, "Remember, I can't read your mind!"

- Never, never take a cheap shot, no matter how easy it would be! No hitting below the belt, and absolutely no ridiculing!

- Don't make a big deal about a trivial issue. If we do, we need to consider why, and then ask ourself, "What am I really after?"

- If you are wrong, admit it. An apology may be all that it takes to conclude what could have been a confrontational moment on a positive note. Saying, "You know, as I think about it, I may be wrong," can successfully disengage a potential conflict. It is pointless to hold on to an opinion, a solution, or an incorrect fact just because we don't want to lose an argument.

- Remember—timing is everything. Discuss a problem or a possible resolution to a problem at a time when everyone is emotionally ready for the discussion—which generally does not mean a formal meeting at 5:00 p.m. on Friday afternoon!

- At some point, everyone fights dirty or may say things that they may regret later. The best advice is to forgive, forget, and get over it. My 17-year-old daughter uses that advice. One day she shared with me an instance at her high school in which one of the other girls said something to her that many would have felt to be offensive. I asked her, "What did you do?" She paused and then said, "I told her that it was okay that she said what she said, and that I would still like to be her friend." She said that the other girl looked somewhat startled, but thought about it for a moment and then said, "Sure, I would like to be your friend if you still want me to be." My daughter said in return, "I forgive you for what you said. Let's just forget it and go on with our life." My daughter said that the "mean girl," as she was known to be, looked almost stunned. Then, she smiled, and that was the end of what could have been a very negative confrontation. I was proud of my daughter. That level of maturity in a 17-year-old is rare. Or, I should say, rare at any age!

- Be sure and give honest and sincere appreciation for the other person's expressed concern or the other person's opinions.

- It is best to talk in terms of what the other person wants or needs and help her or him achieve it to the degree possible—within reason. In other words, we must work diligently to see things from the other person's point of view, and work with the person to create change that will resolve the concern that the other person has.

Rather than jumping in with my own self-made solution to an issue that has seemed to cause the concern, what can I do to be a better problem solver?

Here are some suggestions that will help you to be a better problem solver. They are very simple suggestions, but sometimes difficult to carry out, depending on your personality:

- Remember, as I have learned the hard way, people like good listeners better than good talkers.

- So, one of the best ways to persuade or negotiate is to be a good listener. The other person may resolve the potential conflict on her or his own by talking it out while you listen silently.

- If you see an argument on the horizon, become a good listener instead. Let the other person vent while you listen carefully. You will win many an "argument" that way.

- In other words, when people are speaking loudly, it is best for us to simply listen quietly.

- Have you ever won an argument? Be honest. Have you ever won an argument? We may have thought we won, but it is generally that the other person simply gave up and said something akin to "Oh well" or "I give up." In other words, the only way to get the best of an argument is to avoid it. In the meantime, try your best to make the other person feel important, wanted, or needed, but do it sincerely.

- So, a misunderstanding is never concluded successfully with an argument, but rather with tact, diplomacy, and a sincere desire to see the other person's point of view.

- If another person seems to be intent on "rubbing you the wrong way" and your first instinct is to retaliate verbally, always distrust your first instinctive reaction to the situation. Pause, listen, and think first. Don't say something that you will later regret. It's so much better to avoid a confrontation than to have to apologize later. Sometimes, it is better to simply say in a kind way, "Thank you for your thoughts," and leave it there.

- More than anything else, it is critically important that we control our temper!

- Always work diligently to see things from the other person's point of view. Failure in communication is almost assured if we consider situations or needs from our personal standpoint.

- In resolving a conflict, look first for areas of agreement. Then, you can address the issues that are found on the other side of that coin.

- Always be honest, but not brutally honest! We are not involved in the discussion to offend, but to problem solve.

- Importantly, we must control our initial instinct to give negative responses to questions and concerns. If nothing else at the moment, we can promise to study the other person's ideas carefully.

When I am involved in a discussion that has as its intent the resolving of a concern by one of my clients, I find it very hard to admit that I am wrong.

Most people find it difficult to admit that they may be wrong. But a simple statement by us that admits that we may be incorrect can resolve many a discussion where tensions are becoming higher.

As I stated earlier in this book, it is important to remember that we will never get into trouble by admitting that we may be wrong. A simple statement that might sound something like, "You know, as I think about it, I feel that you are absolutely correct," can defuse a situation where tensions are becoming higher and can resolve a matter of contention into one that can have a positive outcome.

In many instances, it is not the fear of being right or wrong that creates confrontations, but rather the threat to one's self-esteem. It is natural for us to want to be right, and it takes a high level of maturity to admit that we may be wrong!

We must do whatever is possible to help the other person save face. No matter how wrong we might think the other person is, we only destroy ego and potentially good working relationships by embarrassing the other person. Hurting someone's dignity does nothing to resolve issues or solve problems, and dignity is essential to self-esteem.

Have you ever had a salesperson say during a discussion regarding the purchase of a car, "Let's work for win-win!" It could be part of your discussion about adding air conditioning or a better grade stereo system. Well, when you think about it, win-win never really is. There is no such thing. Win-win is really give and take. You have to determine what you are willing to give up in order to make the other person feel that they have won at least to some degree. It doesn't mean "tricking" the other person into thinking they have won, let's say in a discussion about money. It means that losing a little to gain something is perfectly acceptable in the art of interpersonal communication or in persuasion.

In other words, it is important to be creative! Effective conflict resolution or problem solving involves creative thinking—the development of creative ideas.

The Greatest Enemy to Creativity is Criticism

However, the greatest enemy to creativity is criticism. By all means, don't criticize when another person has come up with what he or she thinks is a good idea! Saying "Thank you" and giving sincere appreciation for effort can make creativity blossom, while criticism can destroy it. An atmosphere of appreciation is fertile ground for the creation of good ideas and successful communication.

If you are or have been a parent of a five-year-old child who has come home from preschool or kindergarten with a crayon-drawn picture clutched to her hand to show you what she created in school that day, what did you say? Hopefully, you said, "What a beautiful picture! Please tell me about it!" Even though the picture may be unrecognizable, when the child says, "It's a picture of you, Mommy!" hopefully you said something like, "I didn't know I was so pretty! Thank you sweetheart! Let's put the pretty picture on the front of the refrigerator so everyone can see it!" In light of that positive response, the child will undoubtedly work hard to bring other pretty pictures home, and will probably continue to become more proficient in her artwork!

On the other hand, what if Mom had said, "Oh…what is it?" with a frown on her face? "It's a picture of you, Mommy!" the child proudly says. Mom replies, "Well—it sure doesn't look like me, and besides, you only used two colors. You need to use more to make a pretty picture!" After that negative review, the child would probably hesitate to bring her artwork home to show Mom for fear of more negative responses.

Criticism can destroy creativity. An atmosphere of appreciation and well-founded praise is fertile ground for even greater creativity.

Demand is an Ugly Word

Importantly, in working with business associates (and in raising children), *demand* is an ugly word. It makes rational adults (and children) react irrationally. We can, however, have points that are necessarily, and for important reasons, non-negotiable.

If I Cannot Be Absolutely Sure...

Remember, if I cannot be absolutely sure that I am correct at least 55 percent of the time, on what basis can I tell another person that he or she is wrong?

If you know you are correct in regard to a certain point of contention because you have done your research and have data to prove a point, try to state your findings subtly rather than with fanfare. If you present your findings quietly, people will be more apt to accept what you have to say.

If you find yourself in a new and different situation and you are not sure what may be expected of you, don't try to create a new personality. All personalities complicate communication in their own way. So, do not try to change your personality during discussions or negotiations in an attempt to fit the situation. That usually doesn't work because the new personality isn't really *you*. We should simply control our own personality to our best advantage.

I heard one time that conflict can be an opportunity for growth. How can that be?

No matter how close we are to those with whom we work and play, we cannot be expected to be in agreement on all issues all the time. If we learn to work together positively in resolving conflict, then we tend to grow, and our relationships likewise tend to grow and strengthen as a result. When we learn to recognize the reality of conflicts and are willing to study them with compassionate understanding, it opens avenues to creative problem solving and improved relationships between business associates and significant others in our personal life. If we understand the nature of conflict, and the reasons for it, we can:

- Develop the capacity to recognize and respond to things that matter to the other person.

- Develop calm, non-defensive, and respectful reactions to conflict.

- Develop a readiness to forgive and forget and to move past the conflict without holding resentments and anger.

- Develop the ability to seek compromise and avoid holding grudges.

- Establish our belief that facing conflict directly is the best avenue for both sides (Segal and Smith, 2014, www.helpguide.org).

When I watch the person with whom I am talking, I seem to be able to almost tell what she is thinking. It seems as though the nonverbal aspects of discussions to solve conflicts are important. Are they?

Of course nonverbal communication, which has been discussed earlier in this book, plays an important role in conflict resolution. In fact, in light of the critically high level of influence nonverbal communication has in all forms of interpersonal communication, it plays a very important role in conflict resolution—not only yours, but also the other person's as well.

Read Chapter 5 on nonverbal communication again, and you will see how important that aspect of interpersonal communication can be in conflict resolution. How we or the other person or persons sits or stands, what is done with the hands and feet, and what is done with the eyes all play important roles. They give us clues regarding what the other person is thinking or responding to what we are saying.

When we consider the degree of importance of the nonverbal aspects of communication—from 70 percent to over 90 percent of what is involved in communication—we cannot overlook its importance in conflict resolution. Some of them that apply here include:

- The distance between those involved in the discussion. Standing too close, we may be assumed to be too "pushy," or standing too far away may give the impression that we either don't care or do not want to be near the person. It can make the person with whom we are communicating feel disenfranchised.

- How those involved in the conflict enter the room where discussions will take place—how they walk, make eye contact, and then sit—are all important. Those can appear as being aggressive or caring and compassionate.

- Leaning too far forward in a chair, shoulders hunched forward, can indicate that we have already decided against what is being said.

- Leaning too far back in a chair with hand covering the mouth can indicate hostility toward the speaker's ideas or questioning their logic.

- Legs crossing and uncrossing or heels or toes tapping are all negative clues, perhaps that we are ready to leave!

- What we do with our eyes is a seriously important part of communication, particularly in regard to conflict resolution. Our eyes give us away. Eyes shifting from side to side can indicate, "Why am I here?" Looking out the door, out through the window, at our shoes, or at the ceiling is a strong indicator that we are uncomfortable being in the same room and are seeking an escape route!

- As mentioned earlier, eye contact, per se, when we are talking with another person is also very important. We should look at the other person's face (the nose is a good spot to concentrate on). Do *not* look directly into the other person's eyes. That is generally interpreted as being too intimate, nor should we look below the face. That can be considered inappropriate.

All of those above are very important to consider when we find ourselves involved in resolution of conflict.

So, what are some final suggestions on how to handle conflict and to succeed in conflict resolution?

If I can provide a good summary of ideas that I provide on behalf of my clients who are interested in how to handle conflict, I have found the following to be excellent suggestions by Segal and Smith:

1. **Listen for what is felt as well as what is said.** Attending to the emotions of the person with whom we are speaking as well as their words can give us greater understanding of the intent and meaning of their dialogue with us.

2. **Make resolution of the conflict the priority rather than "winning" or being the one who is "right."** By not concentrating on being the "winner," we can strengthen our relationship with the other person. Most of all we must be respectful of the other person and her or his viewpoints.

3. **Focus on the present.** If we are holding on to grudges based on past resentments or past behaviors, our ability to see the reality of the current situation will tend to be impaired. We must focus on what we can do in the here and now to solve the conflict.

4. **Pick your battles.** Conflicts can not only be troublesome, but also emotionally draining. So it's important to consider whether the issue at hand is really worthy of our time and energy. Maybe I don't want to surrender a parking space if I've been circling for

15 minutes. But if another is available a little further away, arguing over that one space probably isn't worth it.

5. **Be willing to forgive and to say, "I think I was wrong to begin with!"** Resolving conflict is impossible if we are unwilling or unable to forgive or to admit that we may have been wrong. Resolution of a conflict lies in releasing the urge to punish, because the urge to punish can only add to injury and be further emotionally draining.

6. **Know when to let something go.** If we can't come to an agreement, then simply agree to disagree. Remember, it takes two people to keep an argument going. If a conflict is going nowhere, it is appropriate to disengage and move on. Perhaps resolution will occur at an unexpected time sometime in the future. But in moving on, we can still shake hands and smile at the other person. We can still love and appreciate the other person, even though we don't agree!

Note

1. Kathleen Kelley Reardon, *Persuasion in Practice* (Newbury Park: Sage Publications, 1991).

CHAPTER 14

The Communication Conclusion

As the authors of this book, we purposely chose the word *art* in the title *The Art of Communication*. Great art communicates power, passion, emotion, and perspective. It allows the artist to share their deepest emotions while allowing those experiencing the art to perceive it in their own way. The way you communicate throughout your personal or professional life will be one of the greatest factors determining whether you succeed or fail. Your life of communication is your masterpiece, but it is a piece of art that will never be completed.

This book is not intended to be the final word on communication but is, instead, intended to give you a framework for communicating throughout your life. In much the same way that the graduation from an academic experience is called the *commencement* or beginning, as you complete this book, it is merely the beginning of your education and development as a great communicator.

We would encourage you to always stretch and develop your communication muscles. Admire great communicators and emulate them. Learn from poor communicators and avoid their shortcomings.

All of who we are, what we believe, and everything we stand for goes from theory to reality when we communicate. We hope you will communicate with us as you commence your personal and professional journey through life utilizing the Art of Communication.

About Ray H. Hull, PhD

Ray H. Hull, PhD is Professor of Communication Sciences and Disorders and Coordinator of the Doctor of Audiology Program, College of Health Professions, Wichita State University. He was Chair of the Department of Communication Disorders, University of Northern Colorado for twelve years; held administrative posts within the graduate school, being responsible for graduate program review and evaluation both at UNC and Wichita State University for eight years; was the Director of Planning and Budget for the Office of the President for seven successful years at the University of Northern Colorado, responsible for the allocation of over $60 million in state-appropriated funds; has held administrative posts both at the University of Northern Colorado in the College of Health and Human Sciences, the Office of the President, and at Wichita State University through the Graduate School; and is a successful grants person, with over $12 million in competitively funded federal grants.

Background

His background in the fields of communication disorders and the neuroscience of human communication began with his college degree in public speaking, drama, and radio/television broadcast, and then moved into graduate work in disorders of human communication, and then a doctorate in the neurosciences of human communication that involved a combined doctoral degree from the University of Colorado School of Medicine and the University of Denver. He works extensively in coaching and speaking on the art of interpersonal communication in professional life—the nature of interpersonal communication that supports success in one's professional life.

Dr. Hull is past Chair of the ASHA Committee on Communication Problems of the Aging; a past member of the Committee on Governmental Regulations; a member of the ASHA/ETS National Audiology Praxis Advisory Committee; the ASHA Advisory Committee for the project "Upgrading Services to Communicatively Impaired Persons," Bureau of Health Professions; the Advisory, Guidance, and Evaluation Team of the ASHA Project on Satellite Training on Communicative Behavior of Older Americans, Administration on Aging; Vice Chair of the ASHA Audiology Advisory Counsel; member of the ASHA Audiology Advisory Counsel; among other national and state association appointments as found in his CV.

He is or has been consultant and advisor to numerous federal agencies, including the Bureau of Health Professions, DHHS; the National Institute on Aging, PHS; the National Institute of Mental Health, NIH; the Administration on Aging, DHHS; the U.S. Department of Education, Office of Special Education and Rehabilitative Services. He has also been an advisor to Congress, the U.S. House of Representatives Select Committee on Health, Sub-Committee on Health and Long-Term Care; the U.S. Senate

Special Committee on Aging and their Committee on Health, Education, Labor, and Pensions in the areas of health services delivery and disability issues; and the U.S. Senate Small Business Innovation Research Program. He is advisor to the Health Care Financing Administration, DHHS on health and mental health issues. He was also selected by the Bureau of Health Professions, HRSA, DHHS to represent the field of aging on their Council on Disability Rehabilitation. Further, he is advisor to the Bureau of Health Professions, PHS; Health Careers Opportunity Program; and advisor/panelist to the Office of Minority Health, PHS, DHHS; and the Division of Allied Health, BHP, HRSA, DHHS; he has been advisor to the World Health Organization on aging issues; advisor/panelist to the various grants programs of the Office of Special Education Programs (OSEP) of the Office of Special Education and Rehabilitative Services (OSERS); U.S. Department of Education as a member of their standing panel for twenty years prior to an additional three-year term including OSEP, NIDRR and RSA; was a member of the Scientific Merit Review Board of the Veterans Administration Health Services Research and Development Program; and is a current grants panelist for Health Resources and Services Administration, DHHS. He is currently advisor to the Smithsonian Institution, Washington, D.C. on behalf of their Accessibility Program for Children and Adults with Disabilities, and is narrator for the Smithsonian magazine. He is also currently an advisor/consultant on behalf of the American Institute for Research, Washington, D.C.

Dr. Hull has been editorial advisor to the *American Journal of Audiology, Ear and Hearing, The Journal of the American Auditory Society, The Journal of the American Academy of*

Audiology, the *Journal of International Audiology*, and numerous book-publishing companies.

He is sought after as a speaker/presenter and has authored and presented over 300 presentations and workshops across the U.S., Canada, South America, and Europe on the art of communication in professional practice, environmental design, central auditory processing, and hearing rehabilitation for children and adults with impaired hearing. These workshops have as their basis the diagnostic and neurophysiologic aspects of auditory impairment, central auditory processing in adulthood and aging, its physiology and psycho/social impact, techniques for counseling and rehabilitation of those persons, the art and science of grant proposal writing, and the art of interpersonal communication and persuasion in professional practice.

His books include:

- *Hearing Impairment Among Aging Persons*, published by Sage Publications, Beverly Hills, California

- *Rehabilitative Audiology: Part I—The Adult, and Part II—The Elderly Client*, published by Grune and Stratton, Inc., New York

- *Communication Disorders In Aging*, published by Sage Publications, Beverly Hills, California

- He was the invited author of the monograph entitled *The Communicatively Impaired Elderly*, for Seminars in Speech, Language and Hearing, Thieme-Stratton Pub. Co.

- *The Hearing Impaired Child In School,* published by Grune and Stratton, New York

- *Aural Rehabilitation: Serving Hearing Impaired Children and Adults* was published by Singular Publishing Group, San Diego

- *Aural Rehabilitation* published by Chapman-Hall Publishing Co., London

- *Hearing in Aging* Singular Publishing Group

- *Aural Rehabilitation—The Elements and Process For Serving Hearing Impaired Children and Adults* published by Thomson Publishing, New York, 2002

- *Introduction to Aural Rehabilitation*, Plural Publishing, San Diego, 2010

- *Hearing and Aging,* Plural Publishing, 2011

Dr. Hull is the recipient of numerous honors and awards. He was elected Fellow of the American Speech-Language-Hearing Association. He was awarded the Red River Award by the Manitoba Ministry of Health and the Winnipeg League for the Hard of Hearing, Winnipeg, Manitoba, for significant service on behalf of hearing-impaired older adults. He was named the University Distinguished Scholar at the University of Northern Colorado. He was named Distinguished Pioneer in Gerontology by the Colorado Gerontological Society. He was awarded the Public Health Service Award, U.S. Public Health Service, PHS, DHSS for significant service to PHS, Region VIII for research and service on behalf of hearing-impaired older adults. He was also named

Distinguished Scholar of the College of Health and Human Services, University of Northern Colorado. He was awarded the Faculty Achievement Award, College of Health and Human Sciences, University of Northern Colorado, for outstanding scholarly activity and teaching excellence. He was also awarded the Award of Excellence for Outstanding Public Leadership in the Cause of Better Hearing and Speech. He was again named Distinguished Scholar of the College of Health and Human Sciences, University of Northern Colorado, and was awarded the Outstanding Faculty Achievement Award. He received the Distinguished Professor Award at Wichita State University by the University chapter of Mortar Board. He was also awarded the Wichita State University College of Education Teaching Award for Excellence in Teaching and the Emery Lindquist Faculty Award for Scholarship and Teaching. He was awarded the 2001 and the 2006 Professor Incentive Award, Wichita State University.

In 2002, 2003, 2004, 2005, and 2007 he was named to *Who's Who Among America's Educators*. In 2009, he received the President's Distinguished Service Award at Wichita State University. He received the Rodenberg Award for Excellence in Teaching by the Wichita State University College of Health Professions in 2014.

Dr. Hull was educated at McPherson College with a B.A. degree in Forensics, Drama, and Mass Communication; University of South Dakota with the M.A. in Communication and Communication Disorders; and the University of Denver, School of Communication with the PhD in Audiology/Neurosciences. He is an active member of the American Speech-Language-Hearing Association, the Academy of Rehabilitative Audiology, and the

American Academy of Audiology, and holds ASHA Certification both in Audiology and Speech-Language Pathology. He is Fellow of both the American Speech-Language-Hearing Association and the American Academy of Audiology.

ABOUT JIM STOVALL

In spite of blindness, Jim Stovall has been a National Olympic weightlifting champion, a successful investment broker, the president of the Emmy Award-winning Narrative Television Network, and a highly sought-after author and platform speaker. He is the author of 30 books, including the best seller, *The Ultimate Gift,* which is now a major motion picture from 20th Century Fox starring James Garner and Abigail Breslin. Three of his other novels have also been made into movies with two more in production.

Steve Forbes, president and CEO of *Forbes* magazine, says, "Jim Stovall is one of the most extraordinary men of our era."

For his work in making television accessible to our nation's 13 million blind and visually impaired people, the President's Committee on Equal Opportunity selected Jim Stovall as the Entrepreneur of the Year. Jim Stovall has been featured in *The Wall Street Journal, Forbes* magazine, *USA Today,* and has been seen on *Good Morning America, CNN,* and *CBS Evening News.* He was also chosen as the International Humanitarian of the Year, joining Jimmy Carter, Nancy Reagan, and Mother Teresa as recipients of this honor.

Jim Stovall can be reached at 918-627-1000 or Jim@JimStovall .com.